'Naomi writes with such warmth, clarity, and spiritual grounding. Her work creates a gentle, steady place for women carrying the complex intersections of faith, motherhood, and work. She has a rare ability to name the unseen pressures while offering hope, compassion, and practical guidance.'

Anna Mathur, *Sunday Times* bestselling author

'*Christian. Mother. Working.* is a breath of relief for every woman trying to hold the beautiful, complicated tension of motherhood, work, and faith. With honesty and grace, Naomi names the realities that many working Christian mothers juggle and even struggle with – the car-seat naps, the mental load, the quiet guilt – and gently places them under the light of scripture. This isn't a call to perfect the juggle; it's an invitation back to presence, purpose, and the God who meets us in our weakness. Through relatable stories, biblical wisdom, and practical reflection, Naomi offers a vision of working motherhood that is both freeing and deeply faith-filled. For any woman who has ever wondered how to honour her calling at home and beyond, this book will steady your heart and remind you that you are not alone.'

Jo Hargreaves, The Faith Filled Therapist

BRF Ministries

15 The Chambers, Vineyard
Abingdon OX14 3FE
+44(0)1865 319700 | brf.org.uk

Bible Reading Fellowship (BRF) is a charity (233280)
and company limited by guarantee (301324), registered in England and Wales

EU Authorised Representative: Easy Access System Europe –
Mustamäe tee 50, 10621 Tallinn, Estonia, **gpsr.requests@easproject.com**

ISBN 978 1 80039 438 4
First published 2026
All rights reserved

A catalogue record for this book is available from the British Library

Christian.
Mother.
Working.

Your practical,
prayer-filled companion

Naomi Aidoo

BRF
Ministries

Contents

Introduction 6

1 The conflict of the call 16

2 Work and calling in a changing world 28

3 The sacred pause of motherhood 39

4 Being seen in motherhood 52

5 The magnificent in the mundane...................................... 65

6 When motherhood doesn't go to plan 78

7 Parenting beyond the early years 90

8 More than motherhood: identity and faith 103

Conclusion: anchoring our story in God's story 114

Dwell and discern 124

Notes..128

Journal pages 130

Introduction

As I write this, my children are aged two and five. My youngest is at the point where she's dropping her nap but still can't quite make it through the day without having one. This means I've just driven around the local area with her in her car seat waiting for her to drop off (if you know, you know). Now, I'm sitting in my car outside my house with my laptop open, writing my book. A bit of a strange way to start things, perhaps – but then, maybe not at all.

Working mothers worldwide are used to these sorts of scenarios – squeezing in a few emails during a naptime or opening your laptop at the kitchen table once the children are in bed. It's part of the juggle.

Yet often, when we take a glance at social media or pay too much attention to somebody else's highlight reel, we can all to easily find ourselves in the comparison trap. We are constantly exposed to perfectly tidy homes without a toy out of place or day trips where no one is complaining or whining at any point. We can find ourselves wondering how the ever-elusive *they* seem to have everything under control while we feel like we're winging it half of the time.

We know, in theory, that we're all in the same boat. We're told over and over again not to compare our very real lives to somebody else's highlight reel – and yet that thief of joy still finds a way to wriggle in, causing us to question ourselves. Throw in a healthy side of 'mum guilt', and rather than being present *or* productive, we instead find ourselves preoccupied with everybody else's opinions as opposed to our own lives.

As Christians, we have another layer still – the peeling back of what it means to obey God in being present mothers (and wives/partners, where that's applicable) as well as excellence in anything else we are called to, such as our careers, businesses, or otherwise. If we are truly, in everything, to work 'as working for the Lord' (Colossians 3:23), part of our parenting and working lives is exploring what that looks like practically. Again, if we look to social media, there are caricatures of Christian motherhood plastered on our feeds, as well as a sliding scale of what things 'should' look like. I don't believe the word 'should' really has a place in conversations like these.

Christian. Mother. Working. is all about speaking to that very situation – it's a call to unite us, remind us, and equip us. I hope to unite us in the fact that, despite my motherhood and my work looking different to yours, we truly are all in this together. I will remind us that God's power is made perfect in our weakness and that striving for unobtainable perfection isn't what we're called to. Lastly, I aim to equip us with biblical and practical truth which will aid both our prayers and our practice as we carry out this very precious calling.

The days are long, but the years are short

As a parent of young children, I've heard the phrase 'The days are long, but the years are short' more times than I can count. I must admit that they didn't especially help me when I was up all day and night with a baby with silent reflux, nor when dealing with picky eating, potty training, and tantrums. However, recently, for the first time ever, I really understood what people are getting at.

I was at the school gate and one of the mums casually alluded to the fact that my youngest would be starting school next year. At first, I brushed it off thinking she'd got it wrong – I mean, she'd not even had her third birthday yet and so *surely* that didn't make sense? Except, it did, and she does indeed start school in just 18 months' time (at the time of writing, of course).

Suddenly, only having 18 months left with a pre-schooler seems beyond belief. After the past almost six years of having at least one child with me at least some of the time Monday to Friday, the thought of not having that anymore doesn't quite add up.

If you're a parent further along in the parenting journey than I am, you'll know exactly what I mean, and, by God's grace, there are many more milestones to come which right now seem like light years away to me. Moment to moment, however, no matter what stage of parenting you're currently in, certain aspects can truly feel all-consuming.

Before I became a parent, I ran my own coaching business and would share with my audience at the time that I was setting things up 'so that I could work around my child(ren)' and would create certain systems, which I thought would allow me that. However, what I didn't realise pre-children is that I wouldn't just require the *physical* space to work in the way I used to work; I also very much required the mental and emotional space too, which I took for granted until the moment my baby was placed on my chest and my entire life changed forever.

The how, what, why, and who

The plans I'd made before becoming a mother soon came apart at the seams when I realised that all that was previously so important to me, to the point of being almost all-consuming, no longer carried the same weight. What I wrestled with, though, was the fact that I'd spent ten years carving out for myself a career which I was proud of, first as a schoolteacher and then as a business owner. Beyond being simply proud of these achievements, I truly saw myself as being called to the work I was doing then, just as I was called to be my beautiful boy's mother.

So what changed?

Well, frankly, everything and nothing.

I still believed I was called to my work. And I knew without a shadow of a doubt I was called to be the best parent I could be. It was time to find a way in which I could honour a me who was now so multi-faceted and a me who, more importantly, sought to honour he who had blessed me with the life I was leading.

Stepping into the world of parenthood, I knew that I wouldn't be the only one feeling a disconnect. As much as there is a new con-nection with your new baby – which is unlike anything I've ever felt before – there are disconnects many of us will not have experienced in seasons past. A significant one for me was the disconnect between the desires and mindset I had pre-children and those that I adopted once they arrived. I knew I wanted work to feature somehow in my life, but I couldn't quite put my finger on how. Beyond that, though, there were some days when I didn't have it within me to even begin to think about anything other than survival.

When my son turned two and I had the wherewithal to use my creativ-ity a little more, I decided to put together the TIME framework. Its purpose was to support me and anyone else who used it to think about four key strands as they went about their days, weeks, and months: : mindset; milestones; me; and mission. Except, I break it down using the acronym TIME: T – thankful; I – intention; M – me; E – expectant. When I found myself floundering to think about how or where I'd been productive with my day, my framework gave me, and then later all who have gone on to use it, an opportunity to exhale and consider where God would have us be *present* as opposed to simply productive. After all, if we're being present where God intends us to be, an additional side of productivity and push isn't always required. Even in my current season, on most days, I use TIME to give myself a little reset, and I'm so confident in its abilities to help calm the chaos many of us feel in the midst of our busy lives, that the framework is now contained in *The TIME Journal*®, which many women have used and given great testimonials on.

If *The TIME Journal*® is the 'how' (with regards to how, at least, this Christian working mother gets things done), my first book *Finding Flourishing* (BRF Ministries, 2024) is the 'what'. It unpacks what the TIME framework is, goes deeper with the themes the journal touches on, and explains why it's helpful and who it's helpful for. It's scripturally supported throughout and offers the reader a deeper dive into work–life well-being from both a biblical and research-supported place.

Having *The TIME Journal*® as the how and *Finding Flourishing* as the what, *Christian. Mother. Working.* speaks to both the why and, in part, the who. It's important to note, though, that this book stands on its own as something written to encourage you whether you've encountered my previous work or not.

There's a lot of content which fills our bookshelves and our social media feeds about women, about mothers, about working women who happen to be mothers, and about work and business. What's not seen as much, though, is the faith aspect. Don't get me wrong, not every Christian's work is evangelistically pointing to Jesus with its outcomes. That's important and necessary, as we are called to be in the world and not of it (John 17:14–16), but we're still out there – we're still here as what I like to call 'multi-responsible women' knowing that God is to be in and through all we do, even while staring at an overfilled calendar of commitments (both ours and our children's) and an even-more-overfilled laundry basket we still need to get to.

'What does God have to do with any of this?', we might ask ourselves as we're about to log on to a meeting in which we're giving a presentation and just five minutes previously we've got in from the school run to find ourselves sweeping cereal off the floor before a quick mirror check.

But it's a lie to believe that God doesn't see those moments, let alone care about them, and that's what this book seeks to explore as it equips you with the biblical truth, prayerful reflection, and space to pause. In fact, thoughts like these, which I had back when I was 22 and starting out as a teacher, got me thinking about and grappling with the theme of work, seeking to understand how to reconcile my passion for Jesus and what his word calls us to with the things I would be doing day in and day out.

An offering, not a manual

Although my parenting stories may sound familiar to you as you parent young children, or have memories of doing so, I am under no illusion whatsoever that I am the fount of all wisdom when it comes to being a Christian working mother. In writing a book with such a vast and varied audience, it would be ignorant of me to assume I know it all. I don't. In fact, I don't think any of us are 'experts' on Christian working motherhood (except when it comes to knowing our own children), and that's not what this book is about.

It's because I am not an expert that I've invited four wonderful Christian working mothers to weave their wisdom into the pages of this book. Dominique van Werkhoven, Lucy Rycroft, Loretta Andrews, and Rachael Newham all have their own unique stories to tell of Christian working motherhood. You will have your own too. Living, working, and parenting abroad; parenting teens; parenting solo; adoption; stopping paid work for a season to take up the vocation of 'stay-at-home mum'; working and parenting in church ministry; and parenting and working while living with mental illness – these women's words will resonate with you if you currently find yourself in any kind of season which reflects theirs. I am so thankful for their contributions.

Lucy Rycroft is an author of multiple books, both self- and tradition-ally published. In 2025, her book *Be Still: 30 devotions for those who feel anything but* was published by BRF Ministries. She is also the founder of Hope-Filled Family, an online hub of devotionals, courses, and content designed to support realistic family discipleship. Lucy is mum to four children both by birth and adoption.

Dominique van Werkhoven is a writer and speaker. She works closely alongside her husband in the business they run together as well as the non-profit organisation she works with. Dominique is mum to three children.

Loretta Andrews is a music manager and artist development coach, and she has worked in the music industry under a number of guises for many years in both Christian and secular contexts. Loretta is mum to her teenage son.

Rachael Newham is an author and speaker who shares thought-provoking content at the intersection of faith and mental illness, speaking from both lived experience as well as her education in the theology of mental health. Rachael is mum to her young son.

I've introduced each of the contributors here, as their thoughtful and insightful contributions are woven throughout the entirety of this book. When I share quotes of theirs, I'll refer to them by their first names only. Hopefully this brief introduction has given you some context with regards to who the wealth of knowledge and wisdom you're about to dive into has come from.

Each chapter also begins with the story of a woman from the Bible. Like you and me, the women in the Bible found themselves, in their ordinary day-to-day lives, being met with the power of an extraor-dinary God. Not all of these women were mothers, at least not in the traditional sense of the word, just like some of you may not be. However, they were spiritual mothers, caregivers, and leaders in so many other ways that framing each section of the book with their stories seems more than fitting.

To end each chapter, I share some verses for further reflection and then a prayer which speaks to the topic we've just discussed. As I'll touch on more later, writing down my prayers in a journal over the years has been a lifeline for me and if there's anything I know firsthand that faith-filled working mothers need day in and day out, it's prayer. We need prayer for God's power to be made perfect in our weakness (2 Corinthians 12:9); for his perfect peace to saturate our hearts, minds, and circumstances when we're struggling to make sense of any of it (Philippians 4:7); and that we'll receive and act upon the wisdom and guidance we receive in order to raise our children in love and in the Lord (Proverbs 22:6). The prayers are written in first person so that you can pray them yourself, should you find it helpful.

Sandwiched between the biblical account and prayerful proclamation of each chapter, you'll find some of my story interwoven with those of Rachael, Loretta, Dominique, and Lucy, alongside ideas, research, food for thought, and gentle encouragement to guide you in your journey of working motherhood, whatever step you currently find yourself on or season you find yourself in.

After the conclusion, I've shared a series of questions which tie in with the themes in the book. These questions can be used for personal reflection and/or journalling or for discussion in groups. The aim of the questions is that, by reflecting on them, the book becomes not just information to absorb, but truth and wisdom that can be applied.

My hope is that *Christian. Mother. Working.* will be a book you can pick up and put down over and over again – something which you can flick through, finding the parts that speak to your heart and mind based on where you currently are in your journey of working motherhood. There is absolutely no right and wrong when it comes to how we're choosing to raise our children while doing any kind of other work outside of the home, and there is no 'professional parent' – that is, there is no one who's mastered it all. Instead, amid the myriad wise counsel and support you may already have, I pray this book is simply another voice – another helpful addition – along the way.

It feels almost selfish to have the opportunity to write this book in the margin of my children's younger years – an opportunity for me to have on record how I've felt and how I feel. I've noted what God has been saying in this season in the hopes that it encourages and equips you. I also hope that it'll do the same for me when I, by God's grace, find myself in a different season of parenting and find myself wondering what stages gone by were like.

As you read through this book, you'll also be in your own stage of motherhood, whether that be a biological or adoptive parent, a parent-to-be, a step-parent, a foster parent, a spiritual mother, a god-mother, or a caregiving loved one, such as a sister, auntie, or friend. Whatever your season right now, I hope that some of the words on these pages will meet you where you are and provide for you a balm as you pursue all God has for you.

With that, let's pray as we begin.

Prayer

Father God

I thank you that you see every corner of my life: the mountaintops, the mundane, and the messy middle. I thank you that you don't condemn me at any point – not even when I feel I'm at my lowest and laziest – but that you in fact rejoice over me with singing.

I thank you that you're with me always. I pray that you'll give me eyes to see and ears to hear you so that when all I can see are the circumstances which surround me – whether good or bad – I'll first acknowledge you and recognise that because you are for me, nothing and no one can be against me.

There is no need to minimise or maximise anything with you, Lord, as you see and know all anyway. You know the depths of my heart and mind, and I am safe with you. I thank you for that truth.

I pray that my working, my mothering, and everything in between will be as worship unto you, Lord, that I'll know your presence and your peace, which has gone before me.

I pray that the pages of this book might uplift, encourage, and edify me as you see fit, and that you'll bring to mind what you want to illuminate.

In Jesus' name.

Amen

1

The conflict of the call

From scripture: Esther's story

On the shelf above my desk, I have a framed print which every day, in bold black letters reminds me: 'Perhaps this is the moment for which you have been created.' These words are paraphrased from the book of Esther:

> For if you remain silent at this time, relief and deliverance for the Jews will arise from another place, but you and your father's family will perish. And who knows but that you have come to your royal position for such a time as this?
> ESTHER 4:14

The story of Esther is certainly a roller coaster. Plucked out of seeming obscurity, Esther finds herself queen after essentially winning a beauty pageant. This sudden change of status could have most certainly changed her attitude towards those she previously surrounded herself with. However, she remembered who and *whose* she was and, as a result, when the king (Xerxes, Esther's husband) is about to roll out a plot to destroy the Jews, thanks to one of his corrupt officials, Esther presses on in prayer and makes the decision to go in and speak to the king about it – despite knowing her life could be on the line.

The crux of the story comes with the words quoted above, uttered by Esther's uncle Mordecai, who becomes aware of the plan and seeks to speak to his niece, who has been promoted to this position of prominence, that she might do something about it. Esther is of course nervous, but ultimately she speaks to the king and the evil plan is thwarted, thanks to her bravery and courage.

'For such a time as this.'

I wonder whether these words from Mordecai gave Esther the motivation to move or they piled on the pressure, making her feel as though she had no choice. Perhaps it was a bit of both, but whatever it was, her first response was to fast as a form of prayer (Esther 4:15–16). Esther already had favour with the king (2:17–19), yet she wasn't going to allow that to lull her into a false sense of security when walking into what could ultimately have been a death sentence.

Here was Esther, favoured by the king and protected (at least for now) by his provision. She was no longer physically where she used to be. And yet this prompting from her uncle, who was still back there, was all she needed to be reminded of the 'both/and' or her call – to be of service to the king, but also to be committed to her people.

There is no doubt that you also have certain skills and abilities, which have gotten you to where you are today. There are also things we ultimately do by way of second nature when it comes to parenting. However, we'd be remiss to think that our own gifts, abilities, and strengths are *all* we need to focus on when we're in the midst of the juggle we daily face.

Just like Esther, pausing for prayer is where we must begin if we are to find true clarity amid the noise.

Modern mirror

When it comes to parenting and working outside the home, we can feel conflicted about what we're being called to do.

Dominique speaks to this internal conflict in this snippet of our conversation:

> 'When our eldest was born I was working for a Christian non-profit. There was an event that happened in Germany every year, and I was on the team that organised the main stage teaching and the afternoon activities. As part of that role, I was starting to get invited to speak at different events, which I thought was cool as I really love speaking and teaching. People are inviting me to travel to Germany and to Sweden to speak, and then our son was born. I was, like: "Oh, I can't go to all these!" So despite these new opportunities coming up, I was having to turn stuff down. And you know, you're super happy of course to become a mama and you're looking forward to it, while simultaneously realising: "Oh, wait, I hadn't necessarily factored that in – having to say no to certain opportunities."'

From the moment we become mothers, we are faced with a tension that many of us never fully resolve – how do we honour both our families *and* the other work we feel called to do? Whether that work is out of necessity or out of a deep sense of purpose, there's often an unspoken pressure to justify it.

For some, work outside the home is a practical necessity and a way to provide for their families. For others, it's a passionate calling, an extension of the gifts and skills God has given them. And yet, in many Christian circles, there's still an undercurrent of guilt that lingers when women step into paid work while raising children.

Sometimes that guilt is just our own – causing us to wonder what we 'should' be doing, as opposed to tuning into exactly what we're *called* to be doing by our creator.

Lucy puts it beautifully when she says:

> **'When I had my first child, I felt a deep conviction that my role as a mother needed to be my main focus. I left my job, not because anyone told me I had to, but because *it felt like the right decision at the time.*'**

And yet, as Lucy's children grew and different opportunities opened at each step, she found herself stepping back into work in unexpected ways. She reflected:

> **'With each thing which came up, I had to keep asking, "Lord, is this something *you* want me to do?"'**

Lucy and Dominique's stories here are such powerful reminders that the call to motherhood and the call to any other work are not opposing forces. They are not meant to be pitted against one another. Instead, they are two interwoven aspects of our discipleship, shaped by the seasons God places us in. Sometimes, that means pressing pause on professional ambitions. Other times, it means stepping boldly into a career path that was previously unimaginable.

The key is not in choosing one over the other, but rather in seeking God's wisdom in each season.

> Trust in the Lord with all your heart and lean not on your own understanding; in all your ways submit to him, and he will make your paths straight.
> PROVERBS 3:5–6

Whether that path leads us to full-time mothering, full-time working, or a blend of both, the invitation remains the same: to trust that God is leading and to walk forward with confidence rather than guilt, trusting that what God has for us won't pass us by.

In fact, in Dominique's case, she went on to tell me that although she couldn't make that specific event, she went on to speak at one later in the year which provided childcare. God will always make a way if it's what he wants for us.

A theology of calling

Sometimes I wonder if we've made calling more complicated than it needs to be – or perhaps just heavier. Almost as though it's something we have to chase, unlock, or prove.

But what if calling isn't really about career or indeed any specific 'thing' at all? What if it's more about response than achievement?

In scripture, calling usually begins with God's initiative. It does not come as a to-do list or a plan for success, so to speak. Abraham is called to leave his home. Moses is called from a burning bush. Mary is called to carry the Son of God. None of them went *looking* for a calling. They just responded when God spoke.

That idea truly makes me pause, because we often speak about calling as if it's something we must define, as if God is waiting for us to figure it all out. But what if it's actually something we're invited to receive? It makes sense in a very literal way as well. When someone calls our phone, we're not often expecting the call and yet, at that point, we get to choose whether to pick up.

There's a passage in Ephesians 4:1 that doesn't get quoted very often, but I think about it a lot. Paul says: 'As a prisoner for the Lord, then, I urge you to live a life worthy of the calling you have received.' I think about the circumstances Paul was in – chained for the gospel and praying for the Ephesian church. Because of the chapter breaks, we can miss the fact that what comes just before Paul utters these words are the more-often-quoted ones we find in Ephesians 3:20–21: 'Now to him who is able to do immeasurably more than all we ask or imagine, according to his power that is at work within us…'

Paul's train of thought here is that if we're looking to *God* (not our-selves), who can do immeasurably more than we dare to even dream, living a *life* which looks worthy of that is the least which can be expected of us. While this might seem unrealistic or difficult, when we take a step back, it doesn't sound like there's something specific we have to obtain. It sounds more like faithfulness, more like being where you are, with God, and letting that be enough – letting him be enough as he guides you through what's for you, step by step.

Of course, sometimes God does shift us. He opens doors or stirs something new in our hearts and minds. But even then, the core of our calling doesn't change. It's always to him first. It is not to a particular job title or outcome; it's to him.

Romans 12:1 helps us think about it through this lens too: 'Offer your bodies as a living sacrifice, holy and pleasing to God – this is your true and proper worship.' That doesn't sound like something particularly lofty; it sounds earthy, ordinary even. You are called to offer your body – your energy, your choices, your life – to God in whatever season you're in.

So perhaps *that's* actually the invitation here: not to strive for 'a call-ing', but to stay close to the caller; to listen in and to let obedience shape what we do next.

I know that's not always easy when we're juggling home and work. If you're anything like me, you'll wrestle with the pressure to almost prove that we're doing something worthwhile. But maybe we don't need to prove it; maybe we just need to be faithful. Which is of course both harder and simpler than it sounds.

The weight of internalised guilt and the invitation to grace

This internal conflict – the pull between family and work – isn't something we wrestle with alone. It's something so many mothers talk about, both those I know and those I don't, sometimes in passing, sometimes in tears, and they doubt that the right choice is being made. If you've ever found yourself wondering whether you're somehow letting someone down no matter what you choose, you're not alone.

A recent study published in the *British Journal of Social Psychology* found that internalised gender stereotypes massively contribute to feelings of guilt in working mothers. Not just occasionally, but consistently. It turns out that when mothers hold more traditional views about gender roles, they feel far more guilt on days they work longer hours, even if, practically speaking, everything at home is still running just fine.

Interestingly, and perhaps unsurprisingly, fathers holding those same traditional views didn't report the same surge of guilt.[1]

I don't know about you, but I find it strangely comforting to know that this guilt many of us carry isn't because we're doing something wrong. It's often because we've absorbed messages – often quietly and over time – which speak to what we *should* be doing, even when those messages were never ours to carry in the first place. This is why I will forever bang the drum of the necessity to 'shed the *should*', which essentially looks like leaving behind the notion that there is only one right way to do things.

If we dig even deeper, it's not just a cultural thing either. It's human nature to want to do everything well, especially when it comes to the people and the work God has entrusted to us. But when perfection rather than faithfulness becomes the goal, guilt finds an easy foothold.

Another piece of research, published in *MAPP Magazine,* looked at maternal guilt and well-being. It found something that probably won't shock you: that guilt, when left unchecked, chips away at overall happiness. Working mothers who wrestled constantly with guilt experienced higher stress levels and lower job satisfaction. But, happily, the study also found that practising things like self-compassion and gratitude made a noticeable difference.[2]

In other words, when we're kind to ourselves, when we choose grace over guilt, something shifts. We're still the same mothers, doing the same important work, but the weight on our shoulders isn't quite as heavy. And isn't that what Jesus invites us to again and again?

> 'Come to me, all you who are weary and burdened, and I will
> give you rest.'
> MATTHEW 11:28

It's important to ask a question of yourself here. How kind am I being to me? Am I extending to myself the love, patience, and kindness that I do to my children, my spouse, my family, and my friends? If not, why might that be?

I think about Dominique's story – how, when she couldn't travel abroad for work after her son was born, she might easily have fallen into believing she'd missed her chance. But in reality, God opened another door a little later on, one that made space for both her callings as both speaker and caregiver.

It's not always as quick or as clear as we'd like, but the truth is the same: what God has for us won't pass us by.

So maybe, when the guilt creeps in – because it still will, sometimes – the real question isn't 'Am I doing enough?' or even 'Am I doing it right?' Maybe the better questions are 'Am I being faithful with what God has asked of me right now?' and 'Where do I need to cease the striving and shed the *should*?'

There will *always* be tension. There will always be seasons when the balance feels off (which is why I don't believe in balance), the opportunities feel too big, or the parenting demands feel too endless.

The invitation, however, is always to trust. To trust that God sees it all, that he knows the quiet sacrifices no one else claps for. To trust that the way we weave together our family life and our work, however imperfectly, can still be an offering of worship.

To trust that his grace really is enough.

Verses for further study and reflection

There is a time for everything, and a season for every activity under the heavens.
ECCLESIASTES 3:1

He gently leads those that have young.
ISAIAH 40:11

'You are worried... about many things, but few things are needed – or indeed only one.'
LUKE 10:41–42

Whatever you do, work at it with all your heart… It is the Lord Christ you are serving.
COLOSSIANS 3:23–24

Let us not become weary in doing good, for at the proper time we will reap a harvest if we do not give up.
GALATIANS 6:9

Prayer

Father God

I thank you for your love and your faithfulness.

I thank you for the fact that calling isn't especially linear, but that it is broad.

Help me to remember that, especially when I'm putting striving for success ahead of what you say is best.

Help me to worship you, Lord – to worship you as I'm doing the laundry, stacking the dishwasher, running around the playground, and sitting at my laptop.

Thank you for calling me to faithfulness. Help me to heed Paul's call to live a life worthy of the calling I have received – both my calling as mother and the other areas of calling you have given me for this season.

When I feel conflicted, frustrated, and overwhelmed, please remind me, Lord, that you are not the author of confusion. I pray that in those moments, you will give me peace and open my eyes to the very next step you're asking me to take.

Because I know that's all you're asking, Lord – for my obedience in the little that is next, whether or not the fanfare follows.

I pray for pockets of time to seek your face within the parts of my day which feel frantic and full.

I thank you that you long for those times even more than I do and that you are never far off.

I praise you, Lord, for the fact that guilt and shame are not mine to carry. I thank you that you carry me when all I feel I can do is crawl.

Remind me in my day-to-day that your presence is with me and that you are truly all I need.

Amen

2

Work and calling in a changing world

From scripture: Lydia's story

In Acts 16, we are introduced to a woman called Lydia. We don't hear much about the details of Lydia's life – whether she was a wife and a mother or what she did with her spare time. We do know that she was both a reputable businesswoman and a worshipper of God (Acts 16:13–14). Thyatira, the city she was from, was known for its trade, especially in the dying and weaving of purple cloth, which Lydia was in the business of. What I love about Lydia's brief but powerful mention in scripture is the fact that we're made aware instantly that it was on the sabbath that Paul meets Lydia and her conversion happens. Her curiosity and desire for closeness with God had brought this busy businesswoman out of her hustle-and-bustle lifestyle on her day off, in order to pause and pray in the midst of it all. There's certainly a thing or two we could learn from this, isn't there?

Whether this prayer meeting was planned in advance or whether the location was just a prominent place of prayer which many knew about isn't clear. What is clear, however, is that God had certainly purposed for this encounter between Lydia and Paul – for their paths to divinely cross in the midst of all that they were both doing. Towards the end of verse 14, we read: 'The Lord opened her heart to respond to Paul's message' – a timely reminder that it is God who grows faith within us, no matter whose job it is to sow the seeds.

We're also told in the text that other women were gathered there too. Whether or not these women were known to Lydia isn't clear. However, as a woman of wealth, we might infer that she had influence. In our places of work, be they virtual or physical, do we recognise the influence we have on our team and coworkers? As we talk through spreadsheets and invoices, do we also see slithers of opportunity to make mention of God in the midst? This certainly doesn't have to be heavy, but in my experience, even offers to pray for relatives of previous coworkers, who they've disclosed to me as being unwell, have opened up conversations of faith.

You might love your job outside of the home if you have one and feel as if you are undeniably called to it. You might, on the other hand, see it as 'just a job' and wonder why God has you there in the first place. Wherever you land on that scale, may Lydia's story cause you to remember the influence you hold, even in the most unlikely of places. I remember a significant conversation I had with a fellow Christian member of staff while I was teacher. We were talking about a new series of Alpha which had just launched and how brilliant it was. As we were talking, another non-Christian member of staff joined in the conversation stating that 'she almost felt left out' and that 'it sounded so good', which gave us an opportunity to share a little more about what Alpha was and how she could get involved if she wanted to. It can sometimes feel so alien to bring conversations of faith to our places of work. However, in those moments of doubt, it's key to remember that everyone's been created for connection with God, however far off that might seem in reality (Colossians 1:16). That interaction certainly recentred my thoughts to the fact that people are longing for his presence, even without realising it.

Back to Lydia, and we see in Acts 16:15 that she had a household. This might mean that she a husband and children, but in any case we know her influence wasn't only felt outside of her home, but inside it too. Following the receipt of Paul's message, both her and her household were baptised. Moreover, she persuaded Paul and the team who were with him to come and stay at her house.

What I see from Lydia's story is not only the ripple effect of someone with influence, but more significantly, the ripple effect of choosing to wait on God. Lydia made time during the sabbath to attend a prayer meeting, to listen to the message which Paul shared, and to ensure that her whole household heard it too. This all started with personal devotion. The ripple effect this chance encounter had doesn't stop there. We read in Acts 16:40 that when Paul and Silas had been released from prison, they went back to Lydia's house, which had clearly become a place for Christians to meet together, because it states that 'they met with the brothers and sisters and encouraged them'.

Lydia's influence was clear; so was her devotion. If a large portion of your time is spent working outside the home, may you never lose sight of the fact that you are not less than those who choose or have to stay at home with their families (and vice versa). God goes before you wherever you step.

Modern mirror

Not long ago, I was sitting with my five-year-old while he watched an episode of *Bluey*. In case you're unfamiliar with it (although if you have young kids, I highly doubt you are and I'm sure you'll agree with me that it is *brilliant*), *Bluey* is an Australian cartoon that explores family life, friendships, and the everyday world through the eyes of children – well, children who happen to be dogs. In this particular episode, the characters were playing a game of 'mums and dads', each taking on different roles. At one point, one of the characters said, quite matter-of-factly, 'Mums don't work.'

My son turned to me immediately, his forehead creasing in confusion. 'Yes they do,' he said, almost indignantly. 'You work, don't you Mum?'

His innocent certainty made me smile, but it also sank more deeply into my heart than he realised. It was so matter-of-fact that he certainly wouldn't have expected me to mention it here. I felt a wave of quiet pride. Not pride in job titles or achievements, but more simply in the knowledge that, even though I haven't worked full-time since becoming a mother, I have always worked outside of my mothering in some form, and my children know it. They don't just know it; they recognise and celebrate it. They understand that 'work' is part of who I am and not something that stands apart from being their mum. In fact, one of my deepest joys was ensuring that children were invited to the launch of my first book, *Finding Flourishing*, and seeing my children proudly stand up, with my eldest even saying a quick thank you when at the end my husband prayed for me and the message of the book.

As the episode of *Bluey* went on, it thankfully became clear it was challenging some of the stereotypes that mums stay at home and dads go to work. By the end, there was a lovely moment of agreement between the two role-play characters that both mums and dads can work and both can stay at home! Great lessons for our kids to be hearing from their cartoons. However, I wonder if *Bluey* is the anomaly here – whether still, for the most part, certain assumptions about motherhood and work are still prevalent in society. This *Bluey* episode reminded me how important it is, not just for us personally, but also for the next generation, to be intentional in the stories we tell and live. Beyond this, though, it also reminded me how critical it is to root our choices not in expectations or shifting cultural norms, but in faithfulness to God's individual calling on our lives.

When external voices are loud

While we looked at some of those internal pressures in the previous chapter, there's no getting away from the external pressures we can also face, which is what we've begun to discuss here in light of the ripple effect of Lydia's first encounter with Paul's message. Moving beyond biblical times, still with this wider cultural lens – recently, a growing movement known as the 'tradwife' revival has gained attention. The term, short for 'traditional wife', often refers to women who embrace a return to 1950s-style homemaking, focusing full-time on the home, practising submission to their husbands, and rejecting modern feminist ideals. Much of this movement has been amplified through social media, presenting curated images of homemaking perfection. While there is something beautiful about honouring the unseen labour of home life, it is important to remember that traditional gender roles have always been shaped as much by economics and culture as by biblical principle.

When we turn to scripture itself, we find women like Lydia, who became a key figure in the early church. We see Priscilla, a tentmaker alongside her husband Aquila, teaching Apollos the way of God more accurately. We meet the industrious woman of Proverbs 31, who buys fields, trades profitably, and manages her household with wisdom. The Bible honours women working within the home *and* beyond it, rooted not in cultural conformity but in a life of devotion to God.

I'm not saying that men and women must have exactly the same roles within a home. The Bible doesn't even suggest this – Ephesians 5:21–25 is a good place to start if you're interested. However, when scripture is used to keep women small and insignificant, it's important to be clear on the verses that outline how God *actually* used women, including women who worked.

It's important to note here that we're *all* working. Whether we've chosen to be exclusively within the home with our children for a season or there's other paid or voluntary work we've picked up outside of the home – all of it is labour. That labour can be physical, emotional, or mental – sometimes all three. God places no hierarchy on the 'better' way to mother or the best type of choices we 'should' make as mothers as it relates to work.

Given the context of this book, I do want to share some encouragement for those of us working outside of mothering who sometimes feel guilty about it. Research today supports what scripture hints at: that the health of a family does not hinge on whether a mother works outside the home. A long-term Harvard study found that daughters of working mothers were more likely to hold leadership positions and earn higher incomes later in life, while sons of working mothers tended to grow up valuing greater gender equality in family roles.[3] Similarly, a large Gallup survey of over 60,000 women revealed that stay-at-home mothers were significantly more likely to report feelings of sadness, depression, and anger compared to mothers who were employed in some capacity.[4]

Far from being diminished by their work, mothers who are able to bring their whole selves into both their parenting and their wider callings often strengthen their family life, rather than fracture it.

It's startlingly clear to me that, just as I addressed in *Finding Flourishing*, there is no 'should', even when it comes to how we use our time. What matters most is not where or how we work, but the presence of love, stability, and intentionality within the family and the sense of calling we have to carry out what he's asking of us.

As Lucy writes so insightfully:

> **'I stayed home full-time for the early years of motherhood, and I wouldn't change that. But what I've realised as my children have grown is that my work isn't a distraction from them – it's part of what makes me, me. And that's important.**

> If I'm bringing my whole self into motherhood, then I need to recognise that my work is part of that whole. It doesn't diminish my role as a mum, it strengthens it.'

I have found this to be true too. Whether our work is part-time, full-time, freelance, voluntary, or fitted into the margins of family life, it shapes us. It gives us opportunities to influence beyond our homes, to use gifts and talents entrusted to us by God.

It is worth noting too that the way we view motherhood and work is often heavily shaped by the cultures we live in. Dominique captured this so thoughtfully when she shared:

> 'In Austria, you're expected to stay home for at least a year, and many mothers take two. If you go back to work early, it's almost seen as a failure, as if you must be struggling financially or unable to cope with your children. But in the Netherlands, where I first gave birth, it was the opposite – mothers return to work after three months, and staying home longer raised eyebrows. It made me realise just how much of our ideas about motherhood and work are cultural rather than biblical. What God asks of us isn't a one-size-fits-all model, it's faithfulness in whatever calling he's given us.'

Her words capture a truth that is vital for us to hold on to. Whether you find yourself working outside the home by choice, by calling, or by necessity, or whether you are called to focus fully within the home, the most important thing is not the structure of your days, but the posture of your heart before God. He's not asking for conformity to a human ideal, but for obedience, devotion, and stewardship of whatever sphere he has placed us in.

> **Wherever God has called you - be it home, office, classroom, research lab, hospital ward, or somewhere else - your faithfulness there matters.**

The influence you carry, just as Lydia's did, can ripple far beyond what you immediately see. It can touch your household, your colleagues, your community, and your children's understanding of what it means to live a life rooted in Christ.

In a world that tempts us to compare and judge – where some idealise working mothers and others idealise stay-at-home mothers – may we be women who resist such narrow definitions. May we be women who, like Lydia, bring our full selves to our faith, our families, and our work, recognising that God's purposes are not confined to one model or one season.

As we seek to live out our callings, may we also teach our children, in ways spoken and unspoken, that the worth of a mother, like the worth of any child of God, is never measured by whether she works or indeed how she works, but by faithfulness to the one who calls her.

Verses for further study and reflection

'And who knows but that you have come to your royal position for such a time as this?'
ESTHER 4:14

Do not conform to the pattern of this world, but be transformed by the renewing of your mind.
ROMANS 12:2

He who began a good work in you will carry it on to completion.
PHILIPPIANS 1:6

To act justly and to love mercy and to walk humbly with your God.
MICAH 6:8

Each person should live as a believer in whatever situation the Lord has assigned.
1 CORINTHIANS 7:17

Prayer

Father God

I thank you for going before me and paving the way for my life.

I pray you'll help me to walk in your footsteps and that I won't allow the outside noise to veer me off course.

I thank you, Lord, that I don't have to do any one specific thing except to be obedient to you.

Remind me in those moments where jealousy and envy begin to rear their ugly heads, that comparison is the thief of joy.

I pray, Lord, that you'll help me to celebrate my sisters when they're achieving things that I secretly and sometimes not-so-secretly want to be achieving.

I thank you for the work you've given me – all of it. And I pray that you'll be my strength as I commit to it as if working for you.

I pray, Lord, that you will very clearly warn me when I'm veering off course and am stepping outside of your will – remind me in those moments, Lord, that 'good' isn't always God.

I ask, Lord, that the faithfulness and fullness I give to any work I do outside of caregiving will serve as an example to my children – that they'll see it and celebrate it.

I pray for their working lives in the future too, Lord – that they won't be anxious but instead will also know that you've also paved the way for their lives, just like you have for me.

Amen

3

The sacred pause of motherhood

From scripture: Hannah's story

For many women, wherever we are in our career journey, there will
come a time when we know that something in our hearts and minds
has shifted, as we long for a family. This desire can creep up on us
unexpectedly or it can be something which we feel, in a lot of ways,
is a desire we've been born with.

Hannah was no stranger to this desire.

In 1 Samuel 1, we're introduced to Hannah's husband Elkanah and
his two wives, Hannah and Peninnah. We're told almost instantly
that 'Peninnah had children, but Hannah had none' (v. 2). I wonder
if you've ever felt like Hannah might have here – almost as though,
despite having so much, you're identified by what you don't have.
You may feel as though you know you *should* be grateful for where
you are and what you have, but in reality, you feel anything but.

Hannah was here. We read in 1 Samuel 1:5 that Hannah was deeply
loved by her husband, as he would give her a 'double portion' of the
sacrifice he'd make – something reserved only for her. Hannah's desire

for children had put her in a place of pause even before she had any. The desire was all-consuming, and yet we're told in verses 5 and 6 that the Lord had closed Hannah's womb. To add insult to injury, Elkanah's other wife, Peninnah, who was able to bear children, would provoke and tease her about this. When we're in our season of waiting, it can feel a little like that – as though we're being taunted and teased by the others around us having exactly what we're begging God for.

Hannah prays for a son in verse 11, promising she'll dedicate him to the Lord. There is a lot of crying and pleading alongside her prayers, so much so that the priest who happens to be there believes Hannah to be drunk. When Hannah explains what's actually going on, Eli says: 'Go in peace, and may the God of Israel grant you what you have asked of him' (v. 17).

I can't imagine it would have been easy to get up in her own strength at this point, full of faith that *this time* it would be different. Remember, this had been going on for years. And yet, Hannah does get up, she does choose to believe, and we later read that 'the Lord remembered her' (v. 19) and she becomes pregnant.

Such anguish and heartache, much prayer and turmoil, and after what I'm sure felt like forever, she got exactly what she had been asking for.

Many of us will be familiar with a story like Hannah's – this sense that everything else in life is on hold as we prayerfully and practically prepare for a season of motherhood. And then, whether through birth, adoption, fostering, or otherwise, by God's grace we're thrust into this brand new world. And unsurprisingly, the rest of the world, and indeed our lives, which we'd in many ways blocked out, are all still there waiting for us to rejoin them, as though we haven't just ridden the most intense roller coaster!

Modern mirror

Motherhood is often something longed for. It's prayed over, dreamt about, even planned down to the tiniest detail. And yet, even in the most prepared of hearts, it brings with it a pause that can feel both sacred and startling.

For those of us who were mid-climb in our careers or even standing on what felt like a hard-won summit, motherhood can feel like a jolt and a reorientation of everything we thought we knew about work, worth, and worship.

And yet, despite what modern society sometimes whispers, that pause is not wasted. It's not a weakness or a wrong turn. It's often where God does his most tender work.

Even before a child arrives, as Hannah's story reminds us, there can be a sacred slowing, a recalibration of dreams and a shifting of priorities. Perhaps without even realising it, that's where we begin to measure success differently – before children have even arrived.

And when that pause does finally come – whether in a labour ward, an adoption hearing, a foster panel, or a sudden Monday morning of maternity leave – it comes not only with new life, but with an invitation to live differently ourselves.

The pause that changes us

One of the greatest lies we're sold is that any pause means falling behind. That if you aren't constantly producing, posting, achieving, you're somehow slipping further from your 'potential'.

But the truth, borne out in research and real lives, tells a different story.

One study found that mothers returning to work after maternity leave often exhibit stronger 'soft' skills than before: heightened efficiency, sharper focus, and deeper emotional intelligence. They have learned, because they had to, to prioritise, to work wisely, to empathise more richly.[5]

I know first-hand that when you're suddenly fitting a workday around nap times or school runs, you become fiercely efficient with your time, not because you want to rush, but because you have to choose what *really* matters. Simply put, we're almost forced to be 'better' at our jobs because we simply can't afford to waste hours on what doesn't matter anymore.

It's almost as though motherhood sands down the unnecessary, revealing something quieter and more purposeful underneath.

Many other skills are sharpened, some of which can often be over-looked in the workplace: patience, delegation, adaptability, and emotional resilience, to name but a few. These are all traits that any leadership coach would tell you are invaluable, and yet they are forged, often unseen, in the day-to-day trenches of motherhood: in the toddler tantrums, the sibling squabbles, the sudden changes of plan due to unforeseen illness, and the moments we want to scream yet somehow stop ourselves and instead keep on keeping on.

Loretta spoke powerfully of this tension between working and parenting. In our conversation, she shared with me:

> 'People often ask about the work–life balance, and I'm just like: "If you've got any tips, let me know." I think that trying to do it all is an endless thing where you're going to just feel like you do nothing well. Whatever's in front of me at that moment, I try and give it my all, or as much of me that is there.'

There's something so refreshingly honest in that. It is a reminder that maybe the sacredness isn't in balancing everything perfectly, but in being present wherever we are.

Loretta went on to say:

> 'When I'm with my son, then I hope that I'm present and he feels like my attention's on him. And in the same way, when I'm in a workspace, then I try not to be worrying too much about mum things and just do what I can.'

It isn't perfect. It isn't neat. It's real, and that's what life's supposed to be.

> In fact, it's worship, disguised as wiping down counter tops and finishing email drafts. It's holy ground walked out in the everyday.

For Rachael, whose work sits at the intersection of mental health and theology, this sacred pause came not only through parenting, but also through illness. She shared candidly with me how her own mental-health journey forced her to reimagine success:

> 'What I was reminded of by a former boss is that you could lay down in the middle of the room, never do anything else ever again, never lift a finger, and you'd still be as loved by God then as you are now.'

This is a sentence that lingers long after you hear it. I remember having to pause for thought after our conversation and drink those words in. I had to ask myself what I'm about to ask you: do you believe those words? Do you truly believe that, if you just lay down in the middle of the room you're in right now and never got up, God would still love you just as much as he does right now in the hustle and bustle of the day-to-day?

If we truly believe our worth is anchored in Christ, then even when our productivity halts and even when our lives seemingly shrink down to nothing but the next nappy change or hospital appointment, we are still loved beyond measure.

Rachael also shared how her career had shifted, becoming more writing-focused as her mental-health needs changed, allowing her to continue her calling in a way that honoured both her work and her well-being. Her story is such a good reminder that God's call on our lives isn't tied to a singular job title, a full diary, or a highlight reel. It's tied to his unchanging love and his faithfulness to weave beauty even through brokenness.

The skills gained in the pause

Recent studies reinforce what many Christian mothers know instinctively: that pausing for family doesn't erase skills, it enhances them.

As we've begun to discuss, women returning to work after motherhood are often stronger leaders. Research has shown they develop:

- sharper time management (because five minutes can become gold dust)
- greater emotional intelligence (born from endless bedtime talks and toddler negotiations)
- resilience (because surviving the third week of teething should qualify as a management course).

> The ripple effects of a mother's presence, both at home and in work, are far greater than the world sometimes gives credit for.

Allow yourself to remember that this life you're living isn't *for* the world's credit.

God's peace is greater than the world's pressure

Sometimes, especially when the bills still need paying or opportunities slip away while you're out of office, it really can feel like the pause costs too much.

Loretta reflected that, as a single mother, she saw God's provision most clearly when she dared to trust him. She shared:

> **'I've probably seen more evidence of God providing for me than anything else. Particularly financially – even before I was a single mum. He has provided for me in pretty miraculous ways.'**

Provision doesn't always look like lavish abundance. Sometimes it's simply enough 'strength for today, and bright hope for tomorrow', as Loretta quoted from that old hymn. Sometimes it's the grace to do the next right thing, no more, no less.

I remember a conversation I was having with my spiritual director when I was wrestling with how drastically motherhood had changed me. I knew it would change me, of course, but I was really grappling with all we've shared in this chapter. I saw these new sides of me – things like potentially having to reschedule a coaching call if one of my children got sick or having to be much tighter with boundaries and deadlines – and if I'm being really honest, I couldn't see how these things were supposed to *help* the work I was doing outside of caregiving. I saw those things as opportunities for people to view me as flaky and unreliable. I must've sounded especially lost, trying to reconcile the 'me before' with the 'me now'. She gently interrupted me and said something I'll never forget: 'What if your coaching clients are actually set to gain more from you now?'

That was the moment something shifted.

Because that's the lie so many mothers absorb without even realising it: that motherhood narrows us; that the skills we used to have are now somehow less sharp; that who we were before motherhood was more professional, more clear-minded, more capable. It's a lie we absorb, because so often, whether from the rush of hormones or the busy-ness of a schedule, there comes a point where *we decide* that we're not good enough anymore or that we've lost something.

Yes, things are different now and, yes, alongside the deep joy we experience, there's undoubtedly some difficulties too.

But what about the things we've gained? *How could they possibly not* further bolster all that we have to give?

I'd love for there to be a wave of mothers who dare to believe that things can look far different to what the world paints as achievement. There are already many who walk this out and know it, of course. However, when the modern picture that's painted is still that ultimate '#goals' means being super-mum, balancing a baby on a hip, with a home-cooked meal in hand and trailing a list of achievements, it can cause some to question whether the seemingly little we have to offer is truly enough. What if, in God's economy, pausing for motherhood isn't a derailment, but a different kind of achievement?

What if the skills honed at 2.00 am with a restless baby – patience, problem-solving, compassion, for example – are the very things needed for the work he has ahead of us?

What if, as Rachael so powerfully reminds us, our greatest work is not our productivity but our capacity to be loved and to love others well?

It doesn't mean the transition is easy. It doesn't mean we won't sometimes long for the old rhythms or grieve what feels lost. But it does mean we can trust that, in the pause, God is still moving, still weaving, and still writing a story that is good.

Receiving and releasing

To bring it full circle, let's return to Hannah. After all that waiting and all that prayer, Hannah does receive what she asked for: a son, Samuel.

What always strikes me – and sometimes unsettles me too – is what she does next. She doesn't hold on to him tightly or hide him away. She doesn't use the long years of sorrow as a reason to grip him more firmly. Instead, she brings him to the temple – still a child, still so little – and she gives him back to the Lord.

She says, simply:

> 'I prayed for this child, and the Lord has granted me what I asked of him. So now I give him to the Lord.'
> 1 SAMUEL 1:27–28

There's something breathtaking about that kind of faith. It's not just the faith to ask and wait. It's the faith to release too, to remember that what we carry is not ours to cling to.

There's a truth for us here. Motherhood – and the pauses it brings – isn't just about what we hold. It's also about what we learn to hand back. We do this over and over again, not always in grand gestures, but in the choices no one sees: the school drop-offs; the early bedtimes; the job we don't take; the job we do; the gentle hand on a shoulder when we're exhausted; the work email we finally press send on after weeks of hesitation; and the prayer we whisper when there are no more words. These, I believe, are our own small acts of worship. They are our own moments of saying: 'I asked for this. You gave it. So now I give it back.'

We do this not because we're letting go of what matters, but because we're trusting the one who gave it in the first place.

> In the end, the sacred pause isn't just a break from something, but rather an invitation into something deeper. It's a different kind of faith, a slower kind of strength perhaps, and a motherhood that is shaped not just by love, but by surrender. When we stand in that space - somewhere between the asking and the releasing - we discover again that God really is in it all.

In the waiting.

In the work.

In the letting go.

In the grace that holds us through every part.

Verses for further study and reflection

'Be still, and know that I am God.'
PSALM 46:10

'Come with me by yourselves to a quiet place and get some rest.'
MARK 6:31

'In repentance and rest is your salvation, in quietness and trust is your strength.'
ISAIAH 30:15

The Lord is good to those whose hope is in him… it is good to wait quietly for the salvation of the Lord.
LAMENTATIONS 3:25–26

But Mary treasured up all these things and pondered them in her heart.
LUKE 2:19

Prayer

Father God

I thank you for the pause that motherhood so often brings.

To be honest, it often doesn't feel like a pause at all with everything I'm doing – but, also being honest, *that* kind of doing doesn't always feel like it's the right thing.

Thank you, Lord, for the fact there are no rights or wrongs – for the truth and joy there is in the fact that you see every messy part. The things we're struggling to let go of, as well as the things we're looking to reclaim and wondering how.

I thank you, Lord, that none of this is a surprise to you.

I pray, Lord, that you will help me to hold lightly all that you give me – that you'll help me care for and nurture, while recognising that it's you who gives and takes away.

May I never take anything you give me for granted, Lord – even, and perhaps especially when you give me what I *need*, despite it not always being exactly what I want.

I thank you, Lord, that you know best and that, as some parts of my life might feel slowed by motherhood, you're teaching me something new in the slow – you're showing me that it's somewhere I can grow.

Help me to realise that even when I'm not getting through my to-do list as quickly as I'd like, your grace is sufficient, and that when things feel relentless – both fast and slow at the same time – that you are right there with me.

Show me signs of yourself in the midst of the muddle, Lord, I pray.

Help me to remember that none of this is a surprise to you, even when it might feel that way to me, and that the best way for me to remain anchored is by drawing close.

Amen

4

Being seen in motherhood

From scripture: Hagar's story

If there are a group of people who know to expect the unexpected, it's mothers, whether it's navigating children's illness while juggling other responsibilities or something a lot more disruptive, which hits a lot deeper, as we'll explore later in this chapter. Of those in scripture who faced disruption while mothering, there is no one more clearly resonant than Hagar.

We are first introduced to Hagar in Genesis 16, where we find her as matriarch Sarai's slave. We don't read about her heart, her dreams, her gifts, or her interests. Instead, we hear her being spoken *about*. She has no rights herself – no ability to make decisions for herself and not even any say in the decisions being made for her.

To provide a bit of context here, Sarai's husband Abram was told by God that he was going to be made into a great nation (Genesis 12:1–2). This had clearly begun to trouble his wife Sarai, who, very aware of her and her husband's more advanced years, decided to take matters into her own hands. Presumably assuming that God had somehow forgotten about his promise, she decided that, because she was not yet pregnant, Abram should sleep with her slave to produce the promised heir.

Stepping back for a moment here is important, because although she's not the main character in this section of the story, here is Sarai, another woman desirous of the title 'mother', so much so that she changed her plans and disrupted her peace to make things happen in her own time and without a thought to God's timing or the people she would hurt in the process. These events are such solid proof that even 'good' desires don't always mean they're God-ordained. Sarai's actions here give us yet another reminder of the importance of abiding in God's presence and allowing him to direct our steps. Without truly abiding, we may well miss what he's asking of us and, like Sarai did, take matters into our own hands.

Genesis 16:4 tells us that Hagar conceived and began to despise Sarai. Of course, no one would blame Hagar for feeling this way – what was she supposed to do? Stuck between a rock and a hard place, Hagar fled (v. 6). In the very next verse, which I like to think means there was no great delay here, an angel of the Lord was by Hagar's side. One of my favourite things which happens in scripture is when God asks his children where they're going and what they're doing as if he were not omniscient.

> And he said, 'Hagar, slave of Sarai, where have you come from, and where are you going?' 'I'm running away from my mistress Sarai,' she answered.
> GENESIS 16:8

The fact she is addressed by name for the first time gives us further insight into God's perspective on her. God's view on who Hagar was as a person was different to everyone else's, and so was his view on her circumstances. This is why it's a bit of a shock when God tells her to go back to Sarai (v. 9). I wonder if we can relate to how Hagar must have been feeling at this moment. Going back to a place and people she despised – how could this possibly be 'right'? There's so much in the midst of motherhood which doesn't always make the most sense: things which happen and we have no idea why. Hagar's story is a beautiful reminder to us that we don't always need to know if we're following the one who does.

After declaring a promise over Hagar as to who her son, Ishmael, would be, Hagar gives *God* a name:

> She gave this name to the Lord who spoke to her: 'You are the God who sees me,' for she said, 'I have now seen the One who sees me.'
> GENESIS 16:13

Hagar now knows without a shadow of a doubt that she is seen, she is known, and she is loved. Her seeing and knowing that for herself is what changes her perspective. It's not that her circumstances have changed at all. In fact, not only does she have to go back to Sarai, whose mistreatment caused her to flee, but she also has to contend with the fact that her son, who she wasn't planning for in the first place, is going to be 'a wild donkey of a man' whose 'hand will be against everyone and everyone's hand against him, and he will live in hostility towards all his brothers' (Geneses 16:12).

Yet, despite all of this, knowing that she is seen, known, and loved by God is everything Hagar needs to keep going.

A woman pushed to the margins, carrying both life and loss, unseen by those around her, Hagar's story interrupts the narrative with a pause, a wilderness, and a divine encounter that names her pain and gives her hope. That's why her story sits at the heart of this book, because just like Hagar, so many of us find ourselves walking through sorrow while still carrying on. Working. Mothering. Holding it all together… until we can't.

Modern mirror

As I'm writing this, it was Easter recently, and as ever, I'd got the kids a couple of chocolate eggs ready for Easter Sunday. Then, on impulse, I decided to pick up one for my husband too. To be honest, we never do Easter eggs for each other, tending to stick to getting chocolate for the children. But I saw his favourite type of chocolate and made a quick decision.

Roll around Sunday morning, and the eggs had been handed out. All of a sudden, my five-year-old son quietly disappeared. I thought nothing of it at first, until he returned with a handmade card – a folded piece of paper with words like 'Mum', 'Easter', and 'I love you' written in felt-tip and scattered across the page. I gave him a huge hug, thanked him, and smiled, genuinely touched, as I always am by his sweet little notes and cards. And then he said something I won't ever forget: 'Because you remembered everyone but forgot about you.'

Now that *really* caught me off guard. Not because it hurt – in fact, I couldn't stop smiling. It was more because he saw it. The thing we often don't even notice in ourselves. The giving without the glory and the quiet, unacknowledged effort, the remembering of everyone else, which let's face it, sometimes means the forgetting of our own needs, if we're not conscious of tending to ourselves.

I keep thinking about that moment. About how, in his innocence, he mirrored something so many of us carry. The unseen-ness. The quiet corners of both motherhood and work where no one claps and no one posts a picture. The meals made, the emails sent, the prayers whispered, the tears wiped – not all of them from our children's faces either.

God who sees

Hagar's story has always moved me, but more and more I understand it through the lens of God seeing her. Not just the desperation of her circumstances, but the divine interruption of her pain. When no one else called her by name, God did. When no one else saw her, God did.

You are the God who sees me. El Roi.

That name – only used once in scripture – feels weighty. It doesn't just describe what God does, but who *he is*. To me what stands out most is that it was spoken by an Egyptian slave woman in the wilderness, not by a prophet or king. It came from someone on the margins.

So much of our work, and indeed our lives, can feel as though it's lived out in the margins when it comes to motherhood. We're essentially doing the most important work we'll ever do when we're raising our children. And yet, so often, no one sees it. It's certainly rarely met with applause.

I wonder how you feel about that. I must admit that I've found myself feeling frustrated by it more than I'd like to admit. When I've tamed a toddler tantrum organised the children's wardrobe, cooked dinner for everyone during a nap time, or got through the myriad forms the school requires, but it still feels as though I've done nothing 'substantial', I've been known to let it get to me.

We'd be forgiven for thinking this way, and I've certainly learned to give myself grace and remind myself that when it *feels* as though I've not done the things which get the credit, I've still been productive, just in a different (and yet equally important) way.

The real beauty about being seen by God isn't just that we're simply being noticed. It's about the fact that being seen by him means being known by him. It's about God attending to you. His gaze isn't casual or passing. It lingers.

In Exodus 3:7, for example, God says to Moses: 'I have indeed seen the misery of my people in Egypt. I have heard them crying out… and I am concerned about their suffering.'

He sees. He hears. He cares.

And so often, the people he sees most clearly are those no one else notices: women without children, mothers raising them alone, those in grief, those in longing, and those on the edge.

Psalm 34:15 reminds us: 'The eyes of the Lord are on the righteous, and his ears are attentive to their cry.' This is not sentiment, but sustenance.

Rachael said something in our conversation that really gave me pause for thought:

> **'The most important work of our lives is learning how to be loved by God and learning how to love others well.'**

There is something profoundly grounding in that, especially for those of us who feel our value is often tied to what we produce, manage, or hold together. Being seen by God is not about being evaluated. It's about being held.

Loretta offered something similar:

> **'You can feel lonely and you can feel alone and genuinely be both of those things, but because God transcends all of those things, he's with us the whole time.'**

What does it mean for you today to *learn* to be loved by God where you're at in both your motherhood and your work? Perhaps there are some areas where it feels easier for you to experience and feel God's love, and then there are other parts where if you were to be honest with yourself, you're not sure you do experience God's love there. What would it take to change that?

What my son tapped into, without realising it, at least for me on that Easter Sunday, is that sense of noticing, of presence, and of bearing witness to the things that might otherwise go unspoken.

In Luke 7, Jesus encounters a widow who has just lost her son. Jesus sees her: not just the crowd, not just the coffin. Her. The woman who had already lost her husband and was now burying her only son. Moved with compassion, he acts. He doesn't wait for her to cry out. He intervenes because seeing, for God, is always active.

That story is a whisper to all of us: the ones carrying quiet griefs, untended hopes, and the small faithful acts that go unseen. Jesus always sees. And he not only sees, he draws near.

I wonder if there are some of those unseen aspects for you at the moment which cause you to believe that God has simply forgotten. Much like the woman in Luke 7, you've given up believing that there's hope. Remember, God sees even now.

Dominique shared something with me in our conversation, which got me thinking about exposure and vulnerability in motherhood as a whole. She gave birth to her eldest child in the Netherlands and, being fluent in Dutch, she hadn't expected language to be a barrier during labour.

But in the raw, vulnerable moments of labour, she suddenly realised how much she longed for her mother tongue. Not because she didn't understand what was being said around her, but because something in her needed the comfort of familiarity – of home and of words that didn't need translating. It caught her off guard, she said, the sense of exposure and of not quite being able to name things the way she wanted to.

I think that's part of what motherhood does. It opens us up in ways we didn't know were possible. Not just physically, but emotionally and spiritually too. The things that never used to faze us suddenly carry weight. Words matter more and so do presence, safety, and belonging.

The saying 'When a child is born, so is a mother' rings true in more ways than one. Because as we cradle new life, we're also learning how to hold our own – with all the fear and fragility that can come with it.

And yet, even in that, God sees it all.

El Roi. The God who sees.

Not just the child being born, but the mother being formed. Not just the plans we made, but the places where we feel exposed, out of our depth, and uncertain how to say what we need.

It's in that vulnerability that we are perhaps most seen, most known, and most gently held.

We might *feel* unseen, but we're not. God sees. Not only does he see, he also names. He names Hagar. He names her pain. He names her future. He even names her child.

Sometimes, in our unseen moments, what we most long for is not rescue but recognition. Someone to say, 'Yes, this matters, I see you, and you're doing well.' That's the gift of El Roi. Not only that God sees, but that his seeing changes us. It realigns our worth, it reassures our effort, and it reorients our gaze.

I don't think I will ever forget that Easter. Not because of the chocolate, but because of the clarity. The reminder that even when I forget myself, someone is watching. Someone sees. In that instance, it was my child. In every instance, though, it's my God.

The invisible load we carry

If you open social media for half a second, you'll be met with the term 'invisible load', and it's something I've been thinking a lot about lately. I wonder how often you experience it. That constant mental to-do list ticking away in the background, even when we're supposedly resting.

It's the remembering of *everything*. The little things, the snacks needed for the school trip, the name of the new friend your child made – and *their* mum's name – the date of the dentist appointment, the shoes that no longer fit, the looming work deadline, the birthday card that still hasn't been written. I could go on.

It's not just the remembering. It's the anticipating too. The wondering what state everyone will be in when they walk through the door from school, work, or whatever the day has brought them. The quiet decisions made pre-emptively – to avoid tears, to soothe overstimulation, or simply to create some kind of calm.

To be honest, it can be exhausting. But it's also almost impossible to explain. Not because it's too complex, but because it's invisible.

French sociologist Monique Haicault wrote about the way mothers often find themselves always mentally switching between roles – what she called 'perpetual toggling'. You might be physically present at work, but part of your mind is still holding your child's timetable. Or you're folding laundry while mentally composing a work email.

This mental multitasking is something many women recognise deeply, even if they've never had the language for it. I've often likened it to having too many tabs open – not just on your laptop, but in your brain too.[6]

In 2019, a study published in *American Sociological Review* confirmed this, showing that in heterosexual households, women still tend to carry the majority of what's known as 'cognitive labour' – the organising, planning, and keeping-track-of-it-all side of family life. This is the case even when both parents work. Even when the tasks themselves are fairly shared, the weight behind them – the mental and emotional load – often is not.[7]

It's important to say this doesn't mean that all husbands and partners aren't pulling their weight or offering support. Many are and beautifully so. In countless families, the work of home and parenting is a shared dance, carried out with intention and care. My husband and I have a great team dynamic, which I'm truly grateful for. But this research speaks to a pattern, not a universal description. A tendency shaped over time by culture and expectation, not necessarily by fault or lack of effort. And naming it isn't about blame, but about visibility.

Because so much of this – the holding, the anticipating, the quiet scanning of what's needed next – often happens internally. It's not always seen, but it's felt.

I think again about Hagar. About how no one seemed to notice what she was carrying. Not just the child, but the injustice, the dislocation, the sheer weight of doing it all while feeling unseen. The labour wasn't just physical. It was mental, emotional, and spiritual.

But God saw it all.

And maybe that's what we need to hear again. That even when others don't see the cost, God does.

It makes me wonder what would shift if we truly believed God saw the load we carry in our minds? Not just the moments where we finally break down, but the million things that get held in before we do. The stretch, the weight, the invisible.

You are the God who sees me.

It's comforting to me to feel that the seeing isn't only about crisis, but that it includes the quiet calculations of a mother's mind – and counts them holy.

Perhaps that's the invitation of the unseen seasons we might find ourselves in. Not just to endure them, but to allow them to reveal the one who is never distracted, never dismissive, and never late. The one whose gaze is not reserved for the platforms and pulpits, but for the parent in the hallway, the worker at the sink, and the woman in the wilderness.

You are the God who sees me.

And I have now seen the one who sees me.

Sometimes that's all we need to carry on.

Verses for further study and reflection

You are familiar with all my ways.
PSALM 139:3

What is seen is temporary, but what is unseen is eternal.
2 CORINTHIANS 4:18

God is not unjust; he will not forget your work and the love you
have shown.
HEBREWS 6:10

'Your Father, who sees what is done in secret, will reward you.'
MATTHEW 6:4

'Do not despise these small beginnings.'
ZECHARIAH 4:10

Prayer

Father God

I thank you that nothing I say, do, or even think is unseen to you.

While the notion of that might initially feel daunting or overwhelming even, I pray you'll remind me that it is a comfort.

It's a comfort to know that an all-seeing, all-knowing, all-powerful God, sees, knows and, most importantly, *loves* me. Oh, how you love me, Lord. I am so thankful.

I pray, Lord, that when the load feels heavy or I feel too overwhelmed to keep going, I'll be reminded that I don't have to do any of this alone, even if it feels that way sometimes.

You hem me in, Lord – behind and before me, you are there, and so I need not fear.

Forgive me, Lord, for the instances when resentment, frustration, and even anger have bubbled to the surface and caused me to wonder where you are.

Please remind me in those moments, Lord, to pause long enough to know your presence and your peace. May those reminders be enough for me to keep going and extend that same presence and peace to the loved ones you have blessed me with.

Amen

5

The magnificent in the mundane

From scripture: Mary's story

'Nazareth! Can anything good come from there?' (John 1:46). This question, asked by Nathanael, gives us a bit of a picture of what the people of the time thought of the place Jesus was from – the place his mother, Mary, grew up in. Biblical Nazareth was very ordinary. In fact, it was mostly populated by the working poor – those who struggled to make ends meet and worked payday to payday to get by. There weren't very many social elites in Nazareth. To be honest, there wasn't a great deal to note at all.

And yet, in the midst of the mundane – the farming, the carpentry, and the domestic chores – alongside it all, an angel of the Lord appears to an ordinary teenager, in an ordinary town, and calls her 'highly favoured' (see Luke 1:28).

Mary was, as any of us would be, absolutely terrified at the knowledge that the Lord was present – what did this mean? Why me? Have I done something I shouldn't? I'm sure that these were the kinds of questions running through her mind. Mary is told not to be afraid, though, and then the angel reveals why he's there and what it all means.

> 'You will conceive and give birth to a son, and you are to call him Jesus. He will be great and will be called the Son of the Most High. The Lord God will give him the throne of his father David, and he will reign over Jacob's descendants forever; his kingdom will never end.'
> LUKE 1:31–33

These words can so often be reserved for readings we hear at Christmas as we reflect on the birth of Jesus. However, for a moment, put yourself in Mary's shoes. You're a vulnerable Jewish teenager, betrothed to be married and, seemingly completely out of the blue, met with the presence of the Lord for the most extraordinary purpose. How would you have responded? What would you have said and done?

Mary simply asks how – a reminder for us that it's okay to ask God questions. We won't always get answers, but asking God, in the context of our own human limitations, how we're meant to carry out some of the huge things he asks, isn't a problem to God.

The angel explains. And what is Mary's response?

> 'I am the Lord's servant… May your word to me be fulfilled.'
> LUKE 1:38

She was undoubtedly feeling a huge range of emotions at this stage, and yet in the midst of all of them, this ordinary teenager became absolutely anything but – when her ordinary 'yes' was uttered before an extraordinary God.

Modern mirror

Although many of us undoubtedly spend or have spent a vast amount of time in church foyers running around after toddlers or swaying restless babies, there's one Sunday in particular I still vividly remember.

My daughter was just three months old and was overtired, over-stimulated, and entirely uninterested in the idea of the Sunday nap I was desperately trying to get her to take. So I did what many of us have done countless times before: I slipped out to the foyer by the entrance, rocking and shushing and hoping that, somehow, movement would soothe us both.

I was tired and a bit (okay, a lot) frayed at the edges. The week before, I hadn't even made it to church. My three-year-old had a cough and cold, and between tissues and cuddles and the chaos of trying to leave the house with two small children, we'd all surrendered to the sofa. So that Sunday, as I stood in the foyer once again, missing most of the service and straining to catch whatever fragments of the sermon I could, I felt a bit sorry for myself – that sinking feeling you get when the moment you thought you'd have to recharge and reconnect slips between your fingers.

As I paced back and forth with my daughter in my arms, I looked up and I noticed, properly for the first time, what was on the stained-glass windows at the back of the foyer I'd walked in and out of hundreds of times before.

Each of these large stained-glass windows depicted a biblical figure as a child with their parent or grandparent. They are simple scenes, easy to overlook in the hustle of arrival and departure. I'd certainly never really paid attention to what was on them before. But something about that moment with a baby girl resting a bit heavier in my arms, alongside my need to just stand still as a result of the exhaustion, made me stop.

There they were: Eunice (and *her* mother, Lois), Elizabeth and Zecha-riah, Hannah and Elkanah, Sarah and Abraham (parents to Timothy, John the Baptist, Samuel, and Isaac, respectively). But the focus wasn't on their fame. It was on their faithfulness, on their parenting, and ultimately on their legacy.

They weren't just names in scripture. They were people who had raised the next generation. Who had loved and taught and trusted God in the ordinary rhythms of life. Who had wiped noses and soothed fears and spoken promises over tiny lives that would one day echo into history.

It moved me more than I expected. It was exactly what I needed as I wandered and wondered how any of this made a difference. I stood there swaying slightly and thought about how many of us carry this invisible work, the ordinary kind, which never makes the highlight reel. Then I noticed the name below the stained glass – the person these pieces were dedicated to by her family and friends: Mary Chatterton.

I didn't know who she was at the time, but later I found out. Her full name was Mary Ann Brown, and she had lived right there in South London where the church was, at the turn of the 20th century. She ran The Chatterton Arms pub after her husband died, raised her grandchildren, and worked tirelessly for her community. She wasn't a preacher or missionary. She was a landlady, a mother, and a woman of faith who simply kept going.

And that, somehow, felt sacred.

These stained-glass windows weren't especially glamorous. But they did tell a story – one I think many of us live in without always realising its worth.

The magnificence in the mundane.

Because it is magnificent, isn't it? The work of raising a child. Of holding space for your family. Of showing up to work again and again with quiet integrity. Of saying yes to God in a life that may never go viral but is absolutely watched by and celebrated in heaven.

In our conversation, Loretta said:

'I remember going through a long period when I really didn't feel like God was close and I felt quite abandoned. And then I remember listening to a podcast, and they were talking about when, after Jesus had died and risen from the dead, the disciples were walking along and Jesus joined them on the path, chatting to them, but they didn't recognise him. They walked for quite some time chatting to him, and it was only after he'd gone that they realised it was him.

And I remember in this podcast, the point they were making was that sometimes you might think that Jesus isn't next to you or with you, but actually, he's there all along. And it just hit me straight to my heart. I'd been having this really awful time, ranting and moaning and everything, thinking I was moaning to everyone else, and then realised, "Oh, you've been next to me all along." And that really, really strengthened me.'

That's what I imagine Mary Chatterton knew. That God was with her all along – present in the pub kitchen just as surely as in the pew. That his presence didn't depend on the quiet of the sanctuary but could meet you in the bustle of ordinary life.

There's something about mundane faithfulness that makes room for real honesty; that whispers prayers on the school run, trusting you'll still make it to work in time for your 9.00 am meeting, or finds God's comfort in a moment of quiet while the kettle boils after you've been up throughout the early hours feeding your baby.

Dominique understands the value of the mundane. When teaching her children about their varying cultures, she puts it like this:

'In every little touchpoint, there's something… music, books, food. I'm not trying to sit them down and say, "Let's learn about our cultures." But it's in the small things.'

So too is it with faithfulness – it's in the small things. Always.

The washing folded, the TV remote fixed, the lunchboxes packed. The way we keep choosing love, again and again.

Lucy also reflected on work, family, and calling in our conversation together:

> 'At every step it was just trying to be obedient. God would put opportunities in my path, and it was a case of saying, is this something from you, Lord?'

That's what the windows reminded me of that day. Not just the parents in the Bible, but the God who saw them and their children – the same God who sees us. The God who called Abraham while he still lived in tents, who met Hannah in her weeping, who heard Zechariah's doubt and still answered his longing, and who wove legacy through Eunice and Lois long before Timothy preached a single word.

I think I needed that reminder.

I wonder if you need to know it too – that legacy isn't always loud. It isn't always recorded in footnotes and fanfare. Sometimes, it's in the fingerprints left on a church foyer window by a child who just needed a break. Sometimes it's in the story of a landlady who kept going. Sometimes it's in the words we whisper when no one else but God is listening.

Mary Chatterton's story isn't famous. But it is faithful, and faithfulness is how God builds things. She ran a pub, raised her children, supported her community, and stewarded what she had with courage. She was a working Christian mother. She didn't preach from a pulpit, but in a lot of ways, she preached with her life.

I wonder how many of us are doing the same without even realising it.

How many of us are quietly building things – families, homes, businesses, and communities – essentially with our two hands and a huge amount of God's strength?

There is *so* much magnificence in that. In the mother who gets up again after a broken night, in the grandmother who makes a space for her grandchildren to feel safe, and in the one who isn't sure they're doing it right but keeps turning up anyway.

My ego likes to butt against it more often than I'd like to admit, but that's the kind of faith I really want. The kind that lingers in foyers and in kitchens. That rests on stained-glass and sinks into ordinary days and that keeps asking God, 'Are you here too?' and finds, again and again, that he is. He always, always is.

We moved on from that church, but the windows are still there, and their message, which I took with me and continually try to recall amid my mundane, is etched somewhere in me now.

That in the small things – the missed sermons, the rocking babies, and the unnoticed yeses – there is legacy, there is worship, and there is God.

May we know that that's more than enough to keep going.

Finding our wholeness in the middle of it all

Legacy alone doesn't always feel like enough to sustain us. It's a beautiful truth, yes, but one that still has to be lived out in real time. In the middle of packed lunches and postponed dreams and in the push and pull of wanting to be present while also feeling pulled elsewhere.

This is why it's so important to be paying attention – not just to what matters in theory, but to what actually plays out in practice. And here's what I've noticed.

So often we speak about keeping going with both mothering and working as if it requires some sort of inner divide, as if we must tuck one part of ourselves away in order to function well in another. The part that's nurturing must switch off so the part that's productive can rise. Or vice versa. It's subtle, this sense that to be good at any one thing, we have to suppress or sacrifice the other things that make us who we are.

I've fallen for it more times than I can count – the idea that if I want to be truly present with my children, then everything else must go quiet. Or the opposite – if I want to be excellent in my work, then perhaps I must accept being emotionally less available at home.

It's a false dichotomy, and yet one that we're so often conditioned to believe. It is not how God works.

God calls us as whole people. Not compartmentalised versions of ourselves, but integrated ones. We are not machines built to operate in siloed functions. We are image-bearers: complex, layered, capable of compassion and clarity, of strength and softness – all at the same time.

When you read that, what comes up for you, I wonder? Are these truths you believe?

It's no secret that when we try to split ourselves – essentially, when we live divided – it takes its toll. Not just physically, but spiritually too. It becomes hard to hear God clearly when we're constantly muting one voice inside ourselves in order to make room for another. It becomes hard to feel whole when we've told ourselves we can't be.

Something shifted for me recently that brought the fact that God calls us as whole people into focus. It's something really simple, but it's helped me to see where else I'm operating in this black-and-white way of thinking, which I tend to fall into in a number of areas of my life.

I'd been trying to reintegrate exercise into my week. Previously having seasons where I'd work out six times a week, I found myself at essentially zero times (unless you count running around after a toddler). The truth is that getting exercise back into my schedule was something that, for years now, had been pushed aside. I was pregnant, or grieving, or quite frankly too busy, too tired, and as far as I saw it, without enough time. The usual reasons. But instead of waiting for the 'perfect' moment when no one needed me and I had a clear hour to myself (which, let's be honest, rarely comes), I just started. I rolled out my mat, found the workout I was going to do, and got the dumbbells out – in the living room, around my children. They were playing and watching TV, and I just decided it was time to get on with it. But then, the most unexpected thing happened. They put all of that to the side and joined in.

One of them tried star jumps. The other out-planked me (I know!). There was laughter. There was chaos. There were interruptions, of course, but there was joy too. And I realised something as I caught my breath: it's not always a matter of needing to choose. At that moment, I could move *and* be present, I could stretch *and* stay connected.

Maybe that's what wholeness looks like in seasons like these. Not balance, exactly, which suggests the need for neat categories, but moments of overlap. Sacred intersections where God meets us, not in one identity or the other, but in the fullness of who we are.

> Wholeness might not look like everything all at once. It might just look like living undivided. Maybe that's part of what it means to flourish.

The spiritual tension

For many of us as Christian mothers, the tension between work and family is not just logistical but deeply spiritual. We long to be present for our children, to guide them in faith and love, but we also know that God has called us to work, whether that is in ministry, in business, or in some other area.

Yet, in the midst of this, there can be a quiet grief – a sense that we are not quite enough in any one area. Rachael has felt this acutely:

> **'I've had to come to terms with not being the kind of mum I imagined I would be. The reality is that I don't always have the energy to be at every school event or birthday party. My husband takes on more of the parenting load than I ever expected, and sometimes that's hard to accept.'**

For Rachael, learning to mother within her capacity rather than against it has been a spiritual lesson in grace.

As mothers, we can often mistake activity for worth. We equate how much we do, how present we are, how tidy the house is, how well we juggle everything, with our value as women and mothers. But in truth, God is just as present in the slow, still moments as he is in our productivity.

Motherhood, like faith, is built in the daily rhythms of the mundane. It's in the wiping of noses, the making of dinner, the car journeys filled with endless questions. It's in the moments we feel unseen, unproductive, and worn thin. And yet, this is where God delights to meet us.

We don't have to do more to be enough.
We already are.

Verses for further study and reflection

Whatever you do, do it all for the glory of God.
1 CORINTHIANS 10:31

'Now that I… have washed your feet, you also should wash one another's feet.'
JOHN 13:14

Whatever you do… do it all in the name of the Lord Jesus, giving thanks to God the Father through him.
COLOSSIANS 3:17

'May the Lord repay you for what you have done.'
RUTH 2:12

'Whatever you did for one of the least of these… you did for me.'
MATTHEW 25:40

Prayer

Father God

I thank you that although you are extraordinary in every sense of the word, you saw fit to give life to a very ordinary me.

Thank you that you not only gave me life, but breathed it into my bones, causing me too to be able to do some extraordinary things.

When I think about those things, Lord, it almost feels like it didn't come from me, because so often, my life doesn't look like platforms and promotion – it looks like getting breakfast ready, filling in forms, and wiping noses.

I thank you that you don't see any of those things as more significant than the other, Lord, and instead you call all of it good.

Please help me to remember this, Lord, when I feel as though the mundane is meaningless. Remind me of my blessings, Lord – of the fact that even being able to carry out some of those mundane tasks is a miracle.

I thank you, Lord, that you know everything about me – you know my limits and my longings – and you meet me there. I thank you that my calling and capacity aren't pitted against each other – that though there may be times of stretching, yes, your grace is still sufficient and your perfect power will meet my weakness.

May I never forget the seemingly ordinary circumstances you were born into as you began your life on earth as a baby – how you carried Mary as she carried you.

Please remind me that you're carrying me too.

Amen

6

When motherhood doesn't go to plan

From scripture: Naomi's story

The wonderful story of Ruth and Boaz, her guardian-redeemer, is something that would undoubtedly make an excellent modern-day romance novel or film.

Perhaps less rom-com worthy, though, is where Ruth's story begins, with the story of her mother-in-law Naomi. Naomi, her husband Elimelek, and their two sons had left Bethlehem and come to Moab to escape a famine. Ruth 1:1 indicates that this was to be 'for a while' – a temporary part of the plan. What wasn't planned for was for this temporary stop on their journey together to be where it ended for them. We're not told how, but verses 3–5 tell us that Elimelek died and that ten years later, so did her sons. In Ruth 1:5 we're told: 'Naomi was left without her two sons and her husband.'

'How on earth did I get here?' I can imagine Naomi thinking, and perhaps even saying out loud. This wasn't a part of the plan – not how things were meant to go for her and her family. And yet here she was – this faithful follower of God, left as a widower, waiting and undoubtedly worrying about what was to happen next.

In *The Message* translation of the Bible, at the start of Ruth 1:6–7, it says: 'One day she got herself together, she and her two daughters-in-law, to leave the country of Moab and set out for home.'

One day.

We don't know how long she grieved her losses. We don't know how she responded before the 'one day' happened. Nor do we know what her relationship with her daughters-in-law was like. And yet, Naomi hears that the Lord has come through for her people in the provision of food and decides to go home, along with Ruth and Ruth's sister-in-law, Orpah.

Ruth 1:8–13 depicts an intensely painful interaction. Naomi tells her daughters-in-law to 'go back' to their mother's home. She outlines that there's essentially 'no hope' for them with her as a result of her circumstances. She can't provide them with another husband. She sees herself as worthless. Verse 13b very sadly reads: 'It is more bitter for me than for you, because the Lord's hand has turned against me!'

Despite Orpah choosing to go back at Naomi's request, Ruth 'clung to her' (v. 14).

Modern mirror

There are some chapters in our stories that, if we're being honest, we sometimes wish weren't written. They have a way of suddenly unsteadying us when we thought we were on track or at least getting things together. We won't often know when these things will come up either, because that's exactly how grief works. The trauma of being fine one minute, then completely blindsided the next.

I want to give a trigger warning for the rest of this chapter and make it clear that it will mention some hard topics, such as miscarriage, which I know that for a myriad of reasons, we're not all comfortable reading about. If that's you, please look after yourself and feel free to skip to the next chapter.

This chapter is different from the others in format because you'll hear a lot more from our contributors' stories. When loss hits, so often it happens in the middle of everything and everyone else. We all have stories of how the grief gets folded into the day-to-day, hidden in plain sight – because what other choice is there?

This chapter is about the stories that fall through the cracks. The ways we try to keep showing up while holding what feels unholdable. The work of mothering in the midst of mourning, gripping on to the call to trust when nothing makes sense. The God who sees it all.

When I had a miscarriage, it felt, in a lot of ways, like I was living a double life. The outside world kept going – birthday parties, deadlines, nursery runs – and I kept going too. Despite the fact I'd just lost a child and somehow had to still parent my then toddler, and despite the fact this all took place in the middle of a global pandemic and my husband wasn't even allowed into the hospital with me, by and large, I just kept going. Internally, however, I was unravelling.

I had to send messages to family and friends who were waiting to hear about our twelve-week scan. I remember choosing my words carefully, trying not to make it too bleak. I said we were glad that we were recently able to celebrate my eldest's third birthday without yet knowing the news. At that point we were none the wiser and so were still believing for the best. Why do we do that, though, I wonder? Soften the blow, even when it's our own?

There was a dissonance between what I was walking through and how I was expected to walk through it. Like somehow, I felt that grief had to be polite: tidy and time-limited. But real life and real loss doesn't follow that script, of course. Especially for mothers, especially for those in roles of responsibility at work and beyond, it can feel like there's no acceptable space to stop, to not be okay, and even to break.

So instead, many of us do what we've always done: we carry on. We keep working, keep parenting, keep leading, keep hosting. And in the midst of it, we learn to live in layers. Public face. Private ache.

I continually emphasise that we're 'human beings and not human doings', and yet it's much easier to say this than to live it. We don't have to look too deeply into many stories to read tales of women sending 'one last work email', while in the throes of early labour, for example. It can be so hard to truly switch off from our work-based 'doing' when even our bodies are screaming at us to 'be'.

That's why this chapter holds the voices of other women too. Because like Ruth's and Naomi's, so many of our stories are bound up in one another's, woven together through shared grief, grace, and ground. Their journey wasn't linear or neat, but it was real. In that, I believe we find something of our own story – a reminder that God doesn't just see individuals in isolation. He sees us in community, in connection, in the messy middle, where we carry one another and, somehow, keep going.

Loretta, a single mother, shared how Isaiah 54 became a grounding place for her. A place to bring her grief, her questions, and her hope. Verse 13, especially: 'All your children will be taught by the Lord, and great will be their peace.' In her words:

> 'I used to pray that over my son so much. Like, "How can I parent this child by myself?" And then it says, "All your children will be taught by the Lord." I was like, "It's not me that needs to teach him. The Lord will do it himself."'

I found her honesty about capacity moving too. She spoke about how the strength came, not because she had it all together, but because God gave what she needed, when she needed it:

> **'Sometimes you think you haven't got the capacity for something, but God can give you the capacity.'**

This sentiment gave me pause, because so often, when another form comes through from the school which we're told we need to prioritise, while we're simultaneously juggling a big presentation we need to give to our team at work that week, while also making sure everyone has clean clothes and that the eldest's spellings and homework don't slip through the cracks, this notion of 'capacity' isn't something we feel we have very much of. We *daily* need to be reminded of God's strength, so that we find ourselves at his feet before we try another push in our own strength. Before we complain (even internally) about how much we have on our plates, it's so crucial to consider that we were never meant to carry that much on our own.

Rachael also spoke of God being the one to come through, though her context was different. She explained that sometimes she almost feels like a tantruming child coming before God and essentially saying she doesn't like what's happening as she feels herself getting unwell. She said:

> **'Be ruthlessly and unapologetically honest with God about how much it hurts. Doing that before God is powerful. It ushers you closer to him.'**

Even as her life became smaller due to illness, she said, it hadn't stopped her doing meaningful work for God outside of her mothering. It had just changed the shape of it. She spoke of the fact that it became slower and more spacious. That she'd carved out time for more writing than speaking, as well as more time for rest, because she said if she didn't rest, she got ill again quickly.

That honesty was humbling, particularly when she described learning to be okay with not being the kind of mum she once imagined she'd be. There was grief in that, of course, but there was also a new kind of rhythm. She told me:

> 'We've worked out roughly that I can do half a day of activity per weekend… Sometimes it's fine, because it's a weekend where my son wants to just sit and watch a film with me. And we can do that.'

Dominique brought in another perspective again. Her experience of navigating motherhood across cultures and countries revealed a quiet strength, a deep intentionality as she described being in Austria, pregnant again and remembering how disempowered she had felt giving birth the first time in a language that wasn't her mother tongue. And how, this time, she sought out a doula who could speak English. She said: 'I just know now… I'm arming myself.'

I was struck by her clarity:

> 'If it's a stretch to support our family by me attending this event for work, then I'm going to say no. Because I want to go with peace of mind, knowing that my first place of ministry is home.'

It was a theme Lucy touched on too. Reflecting on her own motherhood and work journey, she said:

> 'I think there is still within Christian parents… a desire to put your children first and to prioritise that time that you've got with them. You realise you're the primary spiritual influence in their life.'

And yet still she shared how she has said yes to unexpected roles – freelance writing, charity work, teaching again after 15 years – simply by following what she sensed God was opening up.

Throughout all these stories, I kept hearing a gentle refrain: God sees, God strengthens, and God sustains.

Whether it was Dominique saying, 'I want my kids to feel secure in who they are,' or Loretta whispering that hymn line on weary mornings: 'Strength for today and bright hope for tomorrow.' Whether it was Rachael shifting from platform to pen to honour her healing, or Lucy choosing boundaries that honoured her season, each of these women showed me that sometimes faithfulness doesn't look like getting everything done. Sometimes it looks like trusting God with what we can't.

> There is no single way to mother and no single way to work. But there is, I think, a faithful way to do both: by listening. To our lives and to our limits and most importantly, listening to the God who meets us in the quiet and says, 'I see you, I know, and I'm here.'

Maybe that's what I needed – not a new plan, not a pep talk, just the slow, sacred realisation that even in the hidden, even in the halted, God is still with us. Still faithful, still kind, and still near.

Little loss

It's not always the big, life-defining losses that catch us off guard. Sometimes it's the smaller, more ambiguous ones. The ones you can't quite explain because there's no funeral, no formal goodbye, no clear 'before and after' to mark the moment when something changed.

It's the loss of a version of motherhood you'd imagined. The kind where you thought you'd bake more or shout less. The quiet ache when the feeding journey didn't go how you planned or when school drop-off became a battlefield instead of a bonding moment. The moments when you realise your child is struggling and you can't fix it. Or that you are, and no one has noticed. There's grief there. Even if we're not sure we're allowed to name it.

Ambiguous grief isn't loud, though. It doesn't wear black or speak in hushed tones. It shows up in the pause before you answer, in the way your body tenses when someone asks, 'How's it going?' and you say, 'Fine', even though that's not quite true. It's the invisible weight we carry when we wonder whether this season was supposed to feel different or whether it's just us.

Reminding myself of the fact that we live in seasons where God shows us who or what to prioritise and when has been the single most freeing thing for me in my motherhood so far. When I remind myself that even when my inbox *and* the kid's laundry basket is full, not doing everything at once doesn't make me a neglectful business owner *or* a bad mum. Instead, it makes me human.

Often there's a pressure that runs alongside the busyness and the business of the day-to-day – the myth of the neat ending. The idea that if we're faithful enough, strong enough, and pray hard enough, things will resolve into a tidy bow, that loss always leads to visible fruit, and that we'll be able to point to the 'purpose' of it all and say, 'See? *That's* why.'

But sometimes, we can't and we're not supposed to. Some stories don't tie up neatly and some of the healing and restoration happens beneath the surface, invisible even to us. *That's* why connection to God as our source is not simply a nice thing to have, but a requirement if we're to not only keep going, but also keep growing into all he's calling us to be and do.

When healing is slow and hope hurries

Naomi didn't know what was ahead when she decided to return home. Her grief didn't evaporate when Ruth walked beside her. In fact, she arrived back in Bethlehem and told everyone to stop calling her Naomi – which means pleasant – and instead to call her Mara, meaning bitter (Ruth 1:20). She wasn't hiding her sorrow. She in fact was renaming herself by it.

The story doesn't end there, in bitterness, but neither does it resolve all at once.

I think we need more space for that kind of story. The ones which are still in motion. The ones where healing is happening, but it doesn't always look like we thought it would. Where God is near, but so is the ache. Where hope and disappointment share the same sentence.

There are days when I feel full of vision and purpose and peace. And then there are days I'm not sure what I'm doing at all. Both of those realities can be true, and both can be held. Both can be brought to God – and the days I *actually* bring them to him, as opposed to just knowing that I can in theory while I still try to press on in my own strength, are the days I'll sense the most shift. Not always in circumstance, but in perspective, which is crucial.

The invitation isn't always just to tie up every loose end, but to bring it to the one who weaves loose threads into something beautiful, even if we can't yet see the pattern.

Dominique said something that stuck with me:

> **'I'm learning that God's promises are often fulfilled differently to how I expect. Not less beautifully, just differently.'**

I nodded when she said it. Not because I had a tidy conclusion to offer, but because I knew that feeling. The ache of something good, just not the way you'd planned.

That's the kind of faith I long for, but definitely have a hard time obtaining at points. Not the kind of faith that insists everything will make sense one day, but the kind that trusts even when it doesn't. That says: I still believe you're good, even here, even now, and even (and this part's probably the hardest bit for me) if I'm not supposed to understand or make sense of it this side of eternity.

So, if you're in a season that doesn't feel finished – whether that's loss that isn't quite nameable, an unfulfilled longing, or even a shift you didn't see coming, know this: God sees you. Even in the unresolved. Especially there.

He isn't rushing you to make sense of it. Instead, he's just walking with you through it.

> A bruised reed he will not break, and a smouldering wick he will not snuff out. In faithfulness he will bring forth justice.
> ISAIAH 42:3

Verses for further study and reflection

The Lord is close to the broken-hearted and saves those who are crushed in spirit.
PSALM 34:18

When you pass through the waters, I will be with you.
ISAIAH 43:2

In all things God works for the good of those who love him.
ROMANS 8:28

'The Lord gave and the Lord has taken away; may the name of the Lord be praised.'
JOB 1:21

The Father of compassion and the God of all comfort, who comforts us in all our troubles.
2 CORINTHIANS 1:3–4

Prayer

Father God

I thank you for both the grit and the glory of the resurrection story – that within it, we see a pain which is absolutely unimaginable and unbearable and we also see a hope which is unequivocally unmatched.

I thank you that there's grit and glory in my story too, Lord.

Sometimes it's hard to say thank you for the grittier parts, and I thank you that I can be honest about that with you – that you're not fazed by my tears and tantrums and, in fact, you meet me within them.

It's hard when things don't go the way I thought they would, Lord. Sometimes, it feels unbearable and it's difficult not to continually ask why.

I pray, Lord, that at times like these, I'll be reminded to look up. I'll be reminded that you are a God who is not unable to sympathise with my weaknesses, but has been tried and tested in every way.

I thank you that you meet me in both the pit and the wide-open pastures – help me to see you in each of these moments, Lord, because I must admit that sometimes, I can't see much of you at all.

Thank you, Lord, that your brokenness has made my ashes beauty, and I pray that you'll give me glimpses of that beauty today – no matter what.

Amen

7

Parenting beyond the early years

From scripture: Lois and Eunice's story

In 2 Timothy 1:5, it says: 'I am reminded of your sincere faith, which first lived in your grandmother Lois and in your mother Eunice and, I am persuaded, now lives in you also.'

Although we don't know a huge deal about Lois and Eunice, one thing we do know by way of this verse is that their faith, which was passed on to Timothy, wasn't just taught, it was caught.

This phrase 'now lives in you' struck me again recently. In the ESV translation, the word for this phrase here is 'dwells'. The Greek root which this word/phrase has come from is the word *enoikeō*, which literally means 'to dwell in' or, to expand further, 'to dwell in one and influence (for good)'.

Faith described as dwelling in a person is a faith which, I'm certain, is much more than just lip service. This sort of faith is lived out loud so that those who are on the other side of it don't only experience it through what a person says *about* Jesus, but also because of the life they live *for* Jesus.

This is the kind of faith which Paul was describing Timothy's mother and grandmother as having. Paul not only described this of Eunice and Lois, though, but also of Timothy himself: 'And, I am persuaded, now lives in you also.'

This powerful verse speaks of the opportunity which mothers, fathers, grandparents, and indeed non-biological spiritual mothers and fathers have to pass on a legacy of faith – what a privilege!

As we look at our children and, in many ways, they mirror back to us ourselves as they take in our mannerisms or our features, what of our faith do we see them carrying? What of our faith would we like them to?

Another thing I find striking about this opening to 2 Timothy is the way in which Paul addresses Timothy in verse 2 as 'my dear son'. Very much a spiritual father to Timothy, Paul's heart for him is so abundantly clear, again speaking to the importance of spiritual parents and that much over-used but true phrase 'It takes a village'. Timothy didn't become Timothy by himself. And although he had indeed already grown so much, the journey was not yet finished for him. The next few verses see Paul encourage and admonish Timothy to 'fan into flame the gift of God, which is in you' (1:6).

Parents of children older than mine are clear on the fact that encouragement to keep going and growing for God doesn't stop when they outgrow Sunday school. We know this in theory, but living this out is a whole other story.

There are only four other instances in the Bible which share this *enoikeō* word. One of them is Colossians 3:16 – 'Let the message of Christ dwell among you richly as you teach and admonish one another with all wisdom through psalms, hymns, and songs from the Spirit, singing to God with gratitude in your hearts.' Whether we are birth, adoptive, or spiritual mothers, or otherwise, may God's word dwell richly in us as it shapes our faith and, by God's amazing grace, builds a legacy.

Modern mirror

It feels slightly risky to bring up *Bluey* again. I'm not trying to turn this book into a secret love letter to a children's cartoon (I definitely could). But there's this one episode about 'Show and tell' that caught my attention when my children were watching (okay, and so was I). Bluey tells her mum that when 'grown ups' explain something too much, kids just stop listening. But if you *show* them something – really show it – then they understand.

I think of that a lot when I think of legacy. If there's anyone who embodied a 'show and tell' kind of life, it was Henrietta Mears.

I remember learning about her and reading one of her biographies, *Teacher*, when I too was a teacher, grappling with how my work in the classroom could possibly bear the right sort of eternal weight for the students I'd been given the opportunity to support. A spiritual mother to many, Henrietta never had biological children of her own, yet her life was marked by discipleship, intentionality, and deep, visible love. She founded Gospel Light and Forest Home and taught Sunday school at First Presbyterian Church of Hollywood – not just for a few months, but for decades. During that time, she discipled over 6,000 young people. But more than the scale of what she did, it's *how* she did it that lingers.

Ruth Bell Graham, Christian writer and poet, and founder of The Ruth and Billy Graham Children's Health Center, once said:

> 'I think Miss Mears has the greatest capacity for loving people of almost anyone I know. She taught me a wonderful lesson. Hollywood Christian Group – Miss Mears and I sitting together...

> one of the actresses was called upon for testimony. I sat like the chief of the pharisees, but Miss Mears was muttering "Bless her heart! I just love that girl. She is the dearest thing!" Some of us talk about love. Miss Mears loves.'[8]

It wasn't just her lessons that stuck – it was her love. A love that showed Christ as much as anything she ever taught.

We don't know, of course, but maybe that's what Paul saw in Timothy too. Not just an understanding of the faith, but a dwelling in it – a visible, ongoing, relational kind of faith. One that didn't just stay in synagogue discussions or spiritual theory, but a faith that cooked meals, that prayed out loud, that forgave quickly, that clung to hope. Faith that showed up.

It's easy, I think, to imagine legacy in more sweeping terms, like sermons preached, books written, ministries built, but legacy often also lives in the spaces that no one claps for. In the homes where scripture is spoken gently and in the quiet perseverance of loving the same people over and over again – the precious ones God has entrusted us with.

When it comes to parenting older children – whether biological, adoptive, step, or spiritual – it becomes less about managing and more about modelling.

Lucy shared with me the story of her teenage children deciding to get baptised. It was a big moment, of course, but what struck her most was how they weren't just following what they'd been taught. They were also following what they'd seen. Faith had become their own and it had moved from observation to ownership, from external guidance to internal dwelling.

I think of that Greek word again – *enoikeō*. To dwell in. To influence for good.

That's what we long for, isn't it? Not that our children would merely nod along to what we believe, but that they would encounter Christ for themselves and allow his word to dwell richly within them.

When I think about my own encounters with God as a teenager all the way through to being a young adult, I can almost once again tangibly feel the experiences. Those moments when the Holy Spirit was undoubtedly at work, and I was truly transformed, not just for that moment, but for my life to come. I want my children to experience that – to know that as tempting as it might seem, nothing that the world can offer will ever compare to the true riches found in Christ.

Interestingly, recent data from both the UK and the USA suggests that this kind of legacy isn't just possible – it's happening.

In early 2025, the Talking Jesus report shared that the number of young people in the UK identifying as practising Christians has increased in the last few years. Many of them first heard about Jesus from someone in their own family.[9] Similarly, Barna's 2024 report found that in the USA, Gen Z are among the most spiritually curious generations yet. Despite being raised in an increasingly secular culture, many are open to prayer, the Bible, and church – when it feels real and when it's lived out.[10]

Perhaps that's the point.

It's not about being perfect.
It's about being present.

We're not just handing over information, but rather, offering a way of life. Whether we're doing that as biological parents, spiritual ones, or otherwise, the invitation remains the same – to let faith be seen, not just spoken.

Loretta has said that clinging to Isaiah 54:13 – 'All your children will be taught by the Lord, and great will be their peace' – was more than a comfort for her, it was a conviction. That even in her moments of exhaustion, God was still at work. That her showing up, again and again, mattered – it wasn't all on her shoulders and it never had been.

This sort of legacy – the long-haul kind – doesn't usually announce itself. It's less fireworks and more candlelight: flickering and quiet, but constant.

Lucy described how parenting teens while working brought a different kind of shift too. She spoke about the fact that when her children were small, boundaries were clear and the rhythms were in some ways simpler. In contrast, teenagers are often quieter with their needs. They might *seem* independent, but they still want connection. They still want to be known. So now, legacy looks like staying up a bit later to be around when the door opens. It looks like watching that show with them, not because you love it, but because they do. It looks like noticing the tone of their voice or the length of their silence. It's presence – again. Not perfection, but presence.

There's bravery in that – in deciding to keep engaging when the 'fruit' is slow. In showing up even when you're unsure what difference it makes. Henrietta Mears probably didn't see the full extent of her legacy while she lived, but her fingerprints are everywhere – in leaders she nurtured, in lives she poured into, and in truths she made real.

Before I even became a parent and was a teacher with my own group of teenagers who I'd been entrusted to teach, I recognised the significance of presence and the reality that we pass down things which are not only 'taught', but 'caught' as well.

Henrietta Mears' legacy gave me hope in that regard – that even when (due to the subjects I taught) I wasn't sharing the gospel with my words, I was pointing to him with my actions, and part of that meant being faithfully present in both the good days and the more challenging ones.

Layered legacy

I think about legacy not as a single thread, but as something layered. Something passed on in pieces, through different seasons and some-times, different people entirely.

Not every parent walks this road through biology alone. Some have been entrusted with children through fostering or adoption or as their family blends with another and they become a step-parent. Others become spiritual mothers or fathers, like Paul was to Timothy, deeply invested in lives that didn't begin with them but are still profoundly shaped by their presence.

Parenting in any form is rarely straightforward, but parenting beyond the early years often brings a subtler kind of complexity, especially when you throw work into the mix. It seems as though parenting becomes less about instructions and more about invitations, less about giving answers and more about holding space. And perhaps especially for teenagers, that shift is sharp.

I've spoken with parents of teens who describe this season as both rich and unnerving. The questions are bigger and the silence some-times longer. (To be honest, I remember those moody silences well from my own teenage years.) The decisions feel weightier, and yet the access we once had, to their thoughts, their emotions, their every waking hour, feels suddenly much less guaranteed.

Still, the legacy of presence remains.

It's back to that quote I mentioned at the beginning of the book – 'The days are long, but the years are short.' I'm truly trying to drink in these younger years and enjoy them as much as I can. In the midst of that enjoyment, I'm doing my best with God's leading to sow seeds, which I pray will last for eternity.

Recent research from the Fuller Youth Institute has shown that teenagers with at least five adults in their life who are invested in their faith and well-being, beyond their parents, are significantly more likely to stay engaged with church and personal spiritual practices.[11] It's not about intensity. It's about consistency. Shared meals, open conversations, prayer that is heard and participated in, as opposed to just mentioned. As much as society might sometimes try to push us away from it at times, especially with young people encouraged to spend more and more time behind screens, connection really is key.

It makes me think again of Eunice and Lois. We don't know how long they had with Timothy. We don't know what they got 'right' or what they might have agonised over, but we do know that the kind of faith they lived in front of him didn't evaporate when he turned 13. Instead, it endured.

The same goes for those who parent children they didn't raise from infancy. For adoptive or foster parents, godparents, grandparents, and step-parents, legacy is sometimes about rebuilding trust brick by brick. It's about loving children into a sense of security that allows faith to be possible again. It's not easy, but it's holy work.

If hearing this, while simultaneously grappling with the notion that your work takes up a lot of your time during the week, feels daunting, remember the heart of this chapter – little and often. Small yet meaningful ways to create connection, such as a conversation here or a favourite film there, go a long way when it comes to legacy which lingers and leaves its fingerprints.

A friend of mine, in the journey to becoming a foster parent, told me: 'We don't know if we'll be with them for two weeks or for two years, but we feel confident that our job is to nurture and love them for whatever length of time we're given – that's our part to play.' How powerful. 'That's our part to play.' We are indeed *all* playing our part as we mother and as we work. We're taking what we've been given to steward and trusting that God will meet that morsel of an offering with his magnitude and multiply it.

In keeping with these thoughts around legacy, it's not just about what we pass down, it's about what we stay around for too, for as long as we're given. The long nights, awkward conversations, second chances, forgiveness, and showing up. In truth, whether you're parenting teenagers, guiding spiritual sons and daughters, or walking the slow road of fostering a child into safety, you're building something eternal. Even if it doesn't feel like it.

Those watching us now aren't asking for perfection. Instead, they're asking for real. Real prayer, real trust, and real compassion when we get it wrong. Faith that isn't just recited, but demonstrated. Legacy isn't always loud, but it *is* lasting.

> Sometimes, the most faithful thing we can do is simply stay. Keep listening, keep loving, and keep pointing back to the one who never stops parenting us.

Although we may never see all the impact of our words or presence, that doesn't mean that we stop showing up, and we do so not because it's easy, but because it's faithful. When the word dwells in us – really dwells – it spills over into our conversations, into our homes, and into the hearts of those watching.

As I think about the teenagers and young adults I've loved and mentored over the years, and then, usually for practical reasons like moving home and town, our contact has dwindled, this verse comes to mind:

What, after all, is Apollos? And what is Paul? Only servants, through whom you came to believe – as the Lord has assigned to each his task. I planted the seed, Apollos watered it, but God has been making it grow. So neither the one who plants nor the one who waters is anything, but only God, who makes things grow.
1 CORINTHIANS 3:5–7

While legacy is important, this verse reminds us that we are not responsible for the salvation of everyone we've ever discipled. That's not our job and in fact, playing our part for as long as we're given to play it is okay. God is much bigger than us, and is even more interested in and desirous of people coming to him than we are.

Real truth, real life

Discipleship in the home and with those God has placed around us at the time isn't new, of course. It stretches back through generations – as it did from Timothy to Eunice to Lois – from table to table and from life to life.

Sometimes, it's less formal than we think. It happens in the car, on a walk, in the pause before bedtime. Loretta described it as giving the best of what she had, even if it didn't feel like enough. Maybe that's where God's grace enters – in the gaps between our effort and his movement.

This isn't about producing perfect Christian children, of course. It's about opening our lives in such a way that Jesus can be seen and known through us. It's about leaning on the Holy Spirit for wisdom when we just don't have any more ideas. It's about allowing scripture to shape how we speak, how we forgive, and how we listen.

I keep thinking about something Lucy said – how her work, motherhood, and ministry all weave together. Not tidily, but truthfully. That there are seasons where she's had to say no to some things so she could say a fuller yes to others. That obedience has often looked like small decisions rather than grand gestures.

Really, that's what legacy is made of. Small yeses, quiet faithfulness, and love that lingers. When we doubt whether it's enough, we remember Lois, Eunice, Henrietta, and so many more. Their names may not be printed in every history book, but their legacy lives on. By God's grace, so will ours.

Verses for further study and reflection

Even when I am old and grey, do not forsake me, my God, till I declare your power to the next generation, your mighty acts to all who are to come.
PSALM 71:18

Start children off on the way they should go, and even when they are old they will not turn from it.
PROVERBS 22:6

Be self-controlled and pure… be busy at home… be kind… so that no one will malign the word of God.
TITUS 2:5

'Impress [God's laws] on your children. Talk about them when you sit at home and when you walk along the road, when you lie down and when you get up.'
DEUTERONOMY 6:7

I have no greater joy than to hear that my children are walking in the truth.
3 JOHN 1:4

Prayer

Father God

I thank you for the everlasting legacy you have left – one for both my children and my children's children.

I thank you that as your image-bearer, I will also leave a legacy. I pray that the legacy I leave will be long and full of faith-filled fruitfulness.

I thank you, Lord, for all of those you have entrusted me with – those I've known momentarily and those I have the privilege of loving closely for as long as you give me breath.

I pray for each and every one of them, Lord, that you'll show me what to do and when. That I'll know when to speak and when to be silent – trusting that the example I set will sometimes do the talking without me having to use words.

When it's hard to see those I love not loving you, Lord, help me to be wise and to pass no judgement. Whoever else you put around them, Lord, I pray there will those among them able to offer wise and godly counsel.

I pray, Lord, for those my children will come into contact with across the course of their lives. I pray that there will be faithful mentors, friends, and networks who water the seeds I've planted, and that you'll continue to nurture their growth.

Amen

8

More than motherhood: identity and faith

From scripture: Deborah's story

> 'Village life ceased, it ceased in Israel, Until I, Deborah, arose,
> Arose a mother in Israel.'
> JUDGES 5:7 (NKJV)

When everything had fallen apart – when fear reigned and people stayed indoors – it wasn't a military commander or a king who rose to lead. It was a woman. A prophet. A judge. A 'mother in Israel'.

This one verse, tucked into Deborah's song of victory in Judges 5, frames everything we read in the chapter before. Perhaps it's this lens that helps us see Deborah's leadership most clearly, not just as prophetic or strategic, but somewhat maternal too.

We don't know whether Deborah was a biological mother, but we do know that when she refers to herself as a 'mother in Israel,' she's naming the way she carried the nation and how she rose not to dominate, but to care, to call forth, and to fight for peace.

This is where real maternal power lies: not in limitation, but in legacy; not in soft edges alone, but in spiritual weight too.

Deborah could have easily stepped into the spotlight. She had authority, influence, and people coming to her daily for judgement (Judges 4:5). Yet, when it was time to face Israel's enemies, she didn't appoint herself the victor. Instead, she summoned Barak:

> 'The Lord, the God of Israel, commands you: "Go, take with you ten thousand men of Naphtali and Zebulun and lead them up to Mount Tabor."'
> JUDGES 4:6

She calls him to rise, not because she's incapable, but because she's discerning. This wasn't her battle to lead, it was his. Like any good mother, she knew how to call him forward. This is what maternal leadership looks like: not only recognising the strength we carry in this season, but also understanding the strength we can also impart to others.

When you feel that God has planted an idea in your heart or mind for *his* glory, are you too precious with it? Do you feel that it must be you who fulfils this? Yes, God gives us all individual hopes and dreams, but let's remember, the dreams are his. Perhaps there are others who can partner with you in seeing what God's given you come to fruition? Don't immediately presume it all falls to you.

So, let's check out Barak's response.

> Barak said to her, 'If you will go with me, I will go, but if you will not go with me, I will not go.'
> JUDGES 4:8 (ESV)

Although many people speak about what this verse says of Barak's character, they often overlook what it says about Deborah's. She was clearly a leader who was respected highly. It was no small thing for Barak to ask a woman for help, but he didn't do it for no reason. He knew that having her with him would be of huge value, and she knew the seeds she was sowing as she asked him for that help.

'I will surely go with you,' she says, knowing full well that it will cost Barak personal honour: 'Nevertheless, the road on which you are going will not lead to your glory' (v. 9, ESV).

She wasn't after the win. She was after the work of God being fulfilled. That's what mothers – spiritual, adoptive, and biological – often do.

Deborah sat under the palm (v. 5), offering wisdom and peace, but when the time came for battle, she didn't stay in the shade. She rose and went with Barak.

This part really matters, because how easy would it have been to say, 'This isn't my place,' or, 'God told you, not me.' Deborah didn't cling to comfort; she stepped forward with courage. Whether it's the menial tasks we'd rather delegate or the callings that feel too daunting, maternal leadership is willing to get stuck in.

Though Deborah prophesied the outcome and though her rising brought revival, she didn't centre herself in the victory.

If you are a mother, or someone who leads with maternal strength, it's so important that we know this (and to be honest, I'm speaking to myself here too):

Your nurture does not limit you.

Your compassion doesn't cancel out other aspects of your calling.

Your care is not a smaller path, it's a
deeper power.

Deborah shows us that maternal instinct is not weakness. It is courage, wisdom, clarity, and resolve. It is a strength that raised nations.
And it might just be what revives the 'village' life we've lost.

We'd do well to remember, as we've discussed throughout this book,
that motherhood expands our scope and our potential. It by no
means limits it.

Modern mirror

Research increasingly shows that motherhood doesn't diminish
leadership potential, it actually enhances it. A 2020 study published
in the Harvard Business Review observed that leaders who were
mothers scored higher in resilience, emotional intelligence, and crisis
management than their peers without children. The lived experience of nurturing others, managing competing demands and being
attuned to the emotions of those in your care strengthens, rather than
weakens, your leadership muscle.[12] That lines up with everything I've
observed in myself and in the women I know.

Dominique described it beautifully in our interview. After having her
first child while working for a Christian non-profit, she found herself
saying no to several speaking invitations. Instead of shrinking back,
she eventually discovered a new rhythm:

> 'With the support, this is doable… I had the youngest in the
> carrier with me or my husband took him. I was worried, but
> we could do it. Not everything, but something.'

Something. Not everything. That sounds a lot like wisdom to me.

Lucy echoed this in her story too. Though she initially stepped back from paid work to be at home full-time, she spoke of how her calling didn't disappear:

> 'I would never stop working. There was always something God was putting in my path.'

From running a mums' group to writing about adoption as she began the adoption journey, Lucy's leadership didn't fade; it shifted.

In that shift, we find something powerful, because it's not that our gifts vanish, it's that they deepen.

Rachael spoke vulnerably about what it meant to grieve the version of motherhood she imagined and still show up:

> 'I've had to come to terms with not being the kind of mum I imagined I would be… but there are things I do with my son that are really precious.'

She explained how rest wasn't a luxury but a necessity:

> 'If I don't rest now, I'll get ill later. And that will cost far more.'

That's not stepping back; that's stepping wisely.

Motherhood, in all its forms, teaches us to discern and know what matters most – to sense when to speak and when to be silent; to carry both the grocery list and someone's heartbreak in the same hour.

In other words: to lead.

When we think about identity, not just our function or roles, but who we *are*, this is the truth we must hold tightly to: you are not less of yourself because you're a mother; you are more.

You are more patient than you ever thought possible, more resilient than you ever signed up for, more creative, more responsive, more prayerful, more discerning, more aware of your need for grace, and more generous in giving it.

Reading that might cause you to think: 'All of those things are exactly the *opposite* of what I find myself feeling in the midst of my day-to-day.' You wouldn't be alone in that. I've felt the complete opposite too, and this statement is something I have to continually remind myself of, purely because it's true. Not just subjectively either. Remember that conversation I mentioned I had with my spiritual director which was along these lines? I said to her that essentially, I felt as though I used to be so much more efficient and I wondered if my clients would feel the same about me. The wisdom she shared with me, which I have now passed on to you, are words which have been balm on my more difficult days, because whether we feel it or not, it's true. What we show up with now is more, even when we feel we are less.

> Motherhood may change the shape of your days, but it doesn't shrink the weight of your calling.

Deborah's strength wasn't in denying her maternal nature, it was actually in leaning into it. When we do the same, when we allow our identity to be *formed*, not *frozen*, by the seasons we walk through, we discover a God who doesn't waste anything. Not the sleepless nights. Not the slowed pace. Not the unexpected no's.

It's all part of the story. If it's all part of the story, then maybe we can let go of the pressure to compartmentalise who we were and who we are now. After all, it's not a competition; instead it's an expansion. You're not a different woman, but rather a deeper one.

As you continue walking forward, whether with a baby on your hip or a project on your desk, know this: God sees it all and what's more, he's in it all. He's growing something through you that's rooted, rich, and ready. Not despite your motherhood or despite your work, but because of them.

So, what might that look like in practice?

It might look like setting tighter boundaries on your work hours, not because you're less committed, but because you've learned to honour what's important to you. Like closing the laptop when your working hours are done so you don't miss bathtime, or working a later day so that you get to make your child's morning assembly. Like Lucy, for example, who shared that she only checks her work emails on certain evenings so her teaching work doesn't bleed into family time.

It might look like saying no to what used to be a yes. Like Dominique, who found the courage to be selective about her ministry commitments so that her home remained her first place of peace.

It might even look like adjusting the pace completely, not from failure, but from wisdom. Like Rachael, who honours her capacity with the same reverence as her calling, choosing rhythms that protect both her health and her household.

So here's a gentle encouragement: reflect on what has grown in you *since* motherhood – biological, adoptive, step, spiritual, or otherwise. What strengths are now *more* alive in you than before?

Then ask God how those strengths might serve not just your family, but the world around you, because the truth is: you don't lose your identity in motherhood, you find its fuller shape.

Identity isn't only shaped in quiet, reflective moments. It's also formed in the chaos and the curveballs. In the days that don't go to plan. Motherhood, especially when combined with work, has a way of throwing up those kinds of days more than most.

Expecting the unexpected

As mothers, we truly are pros when it comes to the idea of expecting the unexpected. When I held my interview with Rachael in order to get her wonderful contributions to this book, for example, she was navigating her childminder being off sick and therefore unable to pick up her son from school that very day.

When we are in the midst of motherhood, we very quickly realise that taking things day by day and holding on to plans lightly is crucial. We realise that the dream schedules we had in mind when motherhood was a 'some day', as opposed to a 'today', were all theory without the practical.

I remember being a guest on a podcast in my pre-children days. I'd not long turned 30 and was running my own business. I happily chatted about how I was building my business to work *around* the children I planned to have one day and felt sure I had it altogether.

Cue the confusion a couple of years later, when it felt as though I'd become an entirely new person overnight who now had this other new person to look after. So much to learn and unlearn simultaneously.

Motherhood rarely unfolds exactly as we envisioned or planned for. Thankfully, a huge part of that in my experience is witnessing and experiencing how much more joy, love, and laughter there is in the midst of my motherhood than I ever expected there to be. On the other hand, however, there's also been a lot more tears, tantrums, and tiredness than I expected (my children's and mine!).

Whether it's raising a child with additional needs, navigating cultural expectations, or adjusting to a reality that doesn't match the idealised version we once imagined, there is certainly hardship, which comes with unmet expectations at points in this journey. However, there is also often beauty woven into those broken places.

It's vital, therefore, to plug into God and his never-ending goodness. If we allow ourselves to continually be swayed by cultural norms, people's expectations, and even our own ideals, we absorb so much that we begin to forget what we want and, worse, what God wants for us.

For some mothers, the challenge lies in adapting to a culture different from the one they were raised in. Dominique shared on this powerfully (which I referred to previously), and her experience highlights an important truth: so much of what we believe about motherhood is shaped by the culture around us rather than the gospel. When I first became a mother, I felt the pressure to be fully present at all times, even though I knew I needed space to work, not least as a means of regulating my thoughts and energy. The tension between being 'a good mum' and needing time for focus was something I wrestled with, until I realised that the pressure wasn't coming from God. It was coming from the weight of expectations that didn't belong to me.

Dominique's journey also resonates with many mothers raising children between multiple cultural identities:

'My kids are British, Dutch, Jamaican, and Guyanese. It's not just about what I pass down to them; they have to find their own way of being secure in who they are.'

This echoes our own walk with Christ. We are not meant to conform to a single cultural mould of motherhood. Instead, we are invited to seek God's wisdom and trust that he has called us to raise our children uniquely, in the places and circumstances he has set before us.

The unexpected moments, the times we feel displaced, misunderstood, or like we don't fit the mould, are often where God meets us most intimately. His grace extends beyond cultural expectations, challenges, and societal ideals. In those spaces, we learn that true motherhood is not about fitting a standard, but about walking faithfully in the season we've been given.

Verses for further study and reflection

It is no longer I who live, but Christ who lives in me.
GALATIANS 2:20 (ESV)

For you died, and your life is now hidden with Christ in God.
COLOSSIANS 3:3

You are a chosen people, a royal priesthood.
1 PETER 2:9

We are God's handiwork, created in Christ Jesus to do good works.
EPHESIANS 2:10

Village life ceased… Until, Deborah, arose.
JUDGES 5:7 (NKJV)

Prayer

Father God

I thank you for my motherhood. Although it might look different to others', it is what you have given me to steward.

I thank you for the different lens that motherhood has allowed me to view myself through. Remind me, Lord, that it has expanded me, not shrunk me as I might sometimes feel.

I thank you for the skills you have taught me as you've peeled back more layers and shown me what's beneath.

I pray that from the depth of all I know and have been shown in this season, and indeed in each season of motherhood you've given me thus far, there will be increased fruit, which I can pass on.

I pray that whenever I feel limited, I will first look to you, who is limitless, in order to understand and discern the steps you'd have me take.

I ask, Lord, that you will help me support my children spiritually as well as practically. Remind me to maintain a mindset of eternity when I'm only looking at what's momentary.

I pray that the strengths which are more alive in me now than they ever have been due to becoming a mother, will be used as service in your kingdom, both within my household and beyond.

Amen

Conclusion: anchoring our story in God's story

After this, Jesus travelled about from one town and village to another, proclaiming the good news of the kingdom of God. The Twelve were with him, and also some women who had been cured of evil spirits and diseases: Mary (called Magdalene) from whom seven demons had come out; Joanna the wife of Chuza, the manager of Herod's household; Susanna; and many others. These women were helping to support them out of their own means.

LUKE 8:1–3

Like each of us, each of the women in this passage had their own story. While we might not know the totality of these stories from the little information we have, one thing we do know is that no matter what their start to life had been shaped by, their lives were forever changed after an encounter with Jesus – not simply an encounter though, but also in walking with him.

While we don't read much of Mary Magdalene's past, we do know some of it thanks to verse 2 of the passage above: 'Mary (called Magdalene) from whom seven demons had come out.' If there's anything I've come to learn about the Bible, it's that meaning is woven into every detail.

For seven demons to have come out of this woman, we don't need to think too hard to understand that before her encounter with Jesus, she was in a very dark place. While there's not much else we can liken demon possession to, darkness and heaviness is undoubtedly something all of us have felt at one point or another as we've grappled with the weight of worrying, wondering, and indeed, waiting.

What I love about the mention of the darkness Mary was once held captive by is the fact that it makes Jesus' saving power and healing transformation even greater. I share all of this because that's what I want for each of us to walk away from this book with – an understanding that no matter how deep the depths have been (or indeed are), whether through the loss of a child, the ache of wanting a child so desperately and not having that hope yet fulfilled, the toil involved in turning up time and time again at a job we know is no longer for us, the disappointment in the choices our children have made, or the dissatisfaction we wrestle with in the midst of the mundane moments, Jesus is greater.

That isn't just a platitude either. It's truth. Sometimes, we'll want to wrestle with and bend truth so that it better fits the reality we want to believe in. But just like Mary would have undoubtedly echoed when met with challenge, some of the words I come back to when I wonder if my faith and hope is futile are Simon Peter's when Jesus asks if he's also going to leave him like many of the other disciples did:

> Simon Peter answered him, 'Lord, to whom shall we go? You have the words of eternal life.'
> JOHN 6:68

My story, and indeed my motherhood, may be marked with points of uncertainty and fear. However, I know without a shadow of a doubt that there's no one else who helps, heals, and holds like Jesus. I can give thoughtful ideas, helpful journal and prayer prompts, and share research carried out by people more skilled than I. There is nothing and no one greater that I can point you to – whether you are a biological, adoptive, step-, or spiritual mother – than Jesus.

As a parent, life changes all the time. In the age of AI we're currently walking into, for example, life is changing so rapidly that even some of the best experts can't predict what things will look like in a couple of years. However, one thing which will never, ever change is Jesus.

> God did this so that, by two unchangeable things in which it is impossible for God to lie, we who have fled to take hold of the hope set before us may be greatly encouraged. We have this hope as an anchor for the soul, firm and secure. It enters the inner sanctuary behind the curtain, where our forerunner, Jesus, has entered on our behalf. He has become a high priest forever, in the order of Melchizedek.
> HEBREWS 6:18–20

I trust that as you've walked through my words in this book, as well as the words of Dominique, Loretta, Lucy, and Rachael, you've found solace and strength for the season you're facing. I hope what I've shared here about Mary serves as a reminder that while certain seasons may leave a mark (past, present, or future), none of that is what contributes to the entirety of our reality.

Motherhood and unmasking deeper identity

As we've explored, motherhood well and truly has a way of peeling back layers we didn't even know were there. It's easy to think we know ourselves – our strengths, our flaws, and our limits – until parenting invites us into a version of ourselves we never quite imagined.

Motherhood can require a mindset shift to think of ourselves as image-bearers of Christ as 'mothers' when we only ever hear God spoken of as 'father'. In fact, in my conversation with Dominique, she echoed this same wrestle when she said:

'Obviously the normal image is of God as a Father and I was like well, I'm not a father – but where can I see God reflected in parenting or in motherhood? So there were lots of conversations with God for me – "How have you made me that's going to shape how I mother or how I turn up at work?" There was a lot of research at the beginning and there was a lot of soul searching even in starting a business with my husband or when we worked for a Christian non-profit. There was very much this kind of searching – "Hey God, you've made me 'me', but it doesn't fit into the image of what people are expecting of me in these contexts." I've now got to a place where I don't see God demanding me to be a certain way, but where motherhood is actually a releasing. This wasn't an accident, and he hasn't given me these gifts for nothing – they can be used *in service* of him, of the community, and of the work I do, rather than trying to squish and mould myself into an image that was never me.'

She went on to say:

'And one of my favourite things to talk about or think about is identity – just because I think it comes back into everything and I think so much flows from not only how you see yourself but how you see God.'

I agree with that sentiment around identity and around our differences within even our collective identity as believers. I realise that I write about my experiences of being a working Christian mother through a lens not everyone looks through. That's certainly something motherhood has taught me: that we're all somehow connected and yet deeply unique. The view through my lens may look somewhat different to yours, but it's the variety of perspectives that makes this rich tapestry so beautiful.

As we close this book, there is one more thing I'd like to draw attention to from that perspective of identity and being connected in difference (and that being okay and safe).

Connected in difference

I remember the conversation vividly. I was in my early 20s, deeply immersed in my teaching career and heavily involved in volunteer work through an incarnational ministry project I'd moved across London to join.

'I'm not in a rush to have children,' I exclaimed to some friends one evening. This was perhaps not a surprising thing for a single 24-year-old to say, but it was what I said next that still gives me pause for thought today: 'I think I'm too selfish for kids right now.'

My friends quickly jumped to my defence, arguing that this wasn't true. While I appreciated their kindness, I also knew what I meant. It wasn't, I hoped, that I lacked empathy or care – I had poured myself into teaching and youth work for years, but I understood even then that I needed space. Not just wanted it, but truly *needed* it in order to live and give well. I was anxious that becoming a mother would mean I didn't have that space, and even though it wasn't something I knew how to vocalise at the time, I worried about what that meant for my future motherhood if God chose to bless me with children.

At the time, I labelled it selfishness. Years later, I would come to understand it differently: as an early glimpse of how my neurodivergent mind was wired. A mind that needed time, space, and margin to flourish.

Motherhood didn't erase that need for me. In fact, it amplified it. It was becoming a mother that, for more reasons than I can articulate here, made a way for me to understand myself more. Learning to reconcile the two would become one of the most sacred tensions of my working and parenting life.

When I slowly uncovered the fact I was neurodivergent and it was confirmed in my diagnosis given by a psychologist, I had *so* much clarity. Clarity on what I'd meant in that conversation I had as a 24-year-old, when I had no idea what life would hold. Clarity on what I needed in order to be the best wife, mother, and coach/writer I could be. And most importantly of all, clarity on how my difference was by design and that being fearfully and wonderfully made (see Psalm 139:14) included all of me.

Whether for you it's neurodivergence, a mental illness, a disability, or another kind of difference which motherhood can at times intensify, it doesn't disqualify you from the depth you are known and loved by a God who foreknew it all.

While that might again sound as though it's just words, I'm saying them to myself as much as I am to any one of you reading, because placing our identity in anything other than God (including our work, our family situations, or motherhood itself) can be damaging. When our differences aren't mentioned or seen in the spaces we're in (such as church), saying that we're fully loved and known by God can automatically throw us into defence mode as if our differences make us the exception to this love – and that's simply not the case. Yes, there are some things we'll need to surrender to him – the things within our control which we know are in some way controlling us, and things which God calls sin, of course. The things we can't change or simply control, however, aren't a surprise to God, and being fully known and loved by him isn't in spite of those things, it wholeheartedly includes them.

Sometimes, what our hearts ache for most isn't just to be seen. It's to be invited in and to belong.

One of the things I've come to realise more deeply through motherhood is just how formative true belonging is. Not only for our children, but for us as mothers too. There's something about this particular season of life that gently, or sometimes abruptly, brings to the surface old questions we didn't know we were still carrying.

Questions such as: do I still fit here if I can't do things the way I used to? If I need more rest, if I can't be as present in certain spaces, if motherhood has made me more aware that my capacity has changed, does my place change too?

Motherhood has a way of tendering those questions and of exposing the hidden expectations we've internalised. Some of those expectations come from the culture around us. Some come from church. Some of them, we've simply placed on ourselves. The trouble is, it can be hard to work out where one ends and another begins and even harder to ask those questions out loud when you're already stretched thin.

That's why I find so much comfort in the way Jesus related to people. He didn't begin by asking what they could offer. He began with presence, with nearness, and with welcome. The ones he drew closest weren't the most impressive, they were often the most overlooked.

When I think about the women who walked with Jesus, I'm struck by how deeply he honoured their presence. Not only did he see them, but he included them. They weren't background characters, they were part of his ministry and mission. They belonged.

That reminds me that we, too, belong. In fact, after receiving my diagnosis, one of the very first places I went to were my journals, and the comfort and strength they brought me was so significant, as I recognised that some of the things which could have potentially been difficult in my early 20s as I was re-establishing my faith were actually softened and smoothed over because of the depth of relationship I was forming with Jesus.

Even when we feel unsure of where we fit, even when the pace we used to run at no longer feels sustainable, and even when the things that once made us feel strong now bring us to tears for reasons we can't quite name – we still belong. You still belong.

You are not less faithful because you have seasons you need to slow down. You are not less valuable because your contribution looks different at different points. And you are not less spiritual because you don't always have the time or energy to show up to every meeting or serve in every way.

You are not less.

> **Belonging, in the kingdom of God, isn't earned; it's received.**

In seasons when some aspects seem slower, that truth matters more than ever, because when everything is shifting, when you're relearning who you are and what you need, you need somewhere solid to stand. Somewhere that won't question your worth or your welcome.

Jesus offers that kind of place.

Perhaps, like Mary Magdalene, the most powerful thing we'll ever say isn't a sermon or a strategy or a perfectly curated life. Maybe it's just this:

> **'I have seen the Lord!'**

> **Even here, even now.**

Prayer

Father God

I thank you that it is you who defines me.

Not my desires, nor my deficits, but you.

I thank you that you saw me before the formation of the world and also before I became a mother.

I thank you that you also see me now – in the midst of everything I'm doing, you see who I am.

I thank you that I'm not a surprise to you and that, in fact, it was you who formed me.

I thank you that in every season of my life, including motherhood, you still call me daughter.

Help me to hold that quiet assurance of your support in the face of uncertainty, like Esther did.

Help me to open my heart and home to others, like Lydia did.

Help me to know your nearness when I am broken like Hannah was.

Help me to remember you are the God who sees me when I feel overlooked like Hagar did.

Help me to recognise the extraordinary things which can be birthed out of the ordinary, as it happened for Mary.

Help me to look to you wholeheartedly when my journey doesn't go like I thought it would like Naomi's didn't.

Help me to remember the legacy I'm building for my children every single day I sow into them and may I keep you at the centre of it, just like Lois and Eunice did.

Help me to recognise that motherhood of any kind isn't limiting but empowering, as recall how liberated Deborah was as a spiritual mother.

Ultimately, I thank you, Lord, that in spite of all I am and have been, I can say 'I have seen the Lord', just like Mary did.

May my children know that you are the best thing about me now and always.

Amen

Dwell and discern

I believe offering questions as a way to pause for thought is key. Perhaps it began in my days at youth camp as a teenager. A few weeks after we'd come back from a camp, the initial 'hype' would die down and things would feel normal again. Of course, we can't live in hype, but understanding how we can bring back to the real world some of what we experience in camp comes, I believe, with asking questions, pausing, and digging deeper.

There is something powerful about pausing long enough to let truth settle, and even more so when we allow God to meet us in that pause. These questions are not designed to be rushed through or ticked off. They are here to help you dwell with what you've read and to discern what God might be highlighting in your own story. Take your time. Come back to them whenever you need. Pray and journal through them, and let them open up space for reflection, for honesty, and for hope.

Identity and calling in the midst of motherhood

1 What parts of your identity have deepened – *not* disappeared – since becoming a mother? How can you honour those parts this week?

2 Where do you feel the tension between your calling and your capacity? Take a moment to pray into what needs adjusting.

3 Is there a dream or gifting that feels like it's 'on pause'? What might it look like to re-engage with it gently, in this season?

4 How do you define legacy? In what small, faithful ways are you already building one?

5 What cultural or church expectations about motherhood have you absorbed? Which ones need releasing?

Rhythms, boundaries, and the sacred in the small

1 Where are you currently overextending? What boundary could you lovingly reintroduce – not out of guilt, but out of grace?

2 What's one rhythm or practice that brings you back to yourself and back to God in the busyness? How can you protect it this month?

3 Recall a recent mundane moment that felt meaningful. What did God reveal to you there?

4 When was the last time you felt God's presence in the chaos? Write about it and what it showed you.

5 How does your home environment reflect your values and faith? Is there one small change you could make to create more peace or purpose?

Grief, growth, and the unexpected paths

1 What part of your story has not gone to plan? Have you been able to ask God where he might be working even there? If not, is this something you feel open to trying?

2 Is there a grief you've been minimising or rushing? What would it mean to bring it honestly before God?

3 Which of your limitations has God used for unexpected beauty? Can you name one way that limitation made space for grace?

4 If you're parenting a child with additional needs or navigating a blended/adoptive/foster journey, how can you show kindness to yourself today? When you think about the challenges you're currently facing, is there a way in which you can share the load by asking for help where you need it?

5 What myths about 'the perfect mother' still linger in your thinking? How would God respond to those myths with truth?

Spiritual legacy and intentional discipleship

1 What practices, phrases, or habits from your faith are you already passing on to your children – whether intentionally or not? What would you like to be sharing more of?

2 If someone observed your life this week, what would they 'catch' about your faith? What might you want them to see more clearly?

3 Is there a young person outside of your immediate family you could spiritually encourage this month? What would it look like to show up for them?

4 How might you make room for both truth and tenderness when speaking about faith in your home?

5 What does 'faithfulness over fanfare' look like in your current season? How can you celebrate quiet obedience today?

Notes

1   Lianne Aarntzen, Belle Derks, Elianne van Steenbergen, and Tanja van der Lippe, 'When work–family guilt becomes a women's issue: internalized gender stereotypes predict high guilt in working mothers but low guilt in working fathers', *British Journal of Social Psychology 62:1 (2023)*, pp. 12–29.

2   Frawn Morgan, 'Improving well-being in working mothers: well-being levels and intervention to mitigate the negative impact of maternal guilt' (2023, Doctoral dissertation, Northeastern University). Frawn Morgan, 'Guilt and its intersection with well-being: implications for working mothers, their families, and organizations', **mappmagazine.com/articles/working-mothers**.

3   'Having a working mother is good for you', Harvard Business School press release, 18 May 2015, **hbs.edu/news/releases/Pages/having-working-mother.aspx**

4   Dr Andrew Gottlieb, 'Gallup survey shows stay-at-home moms suffer more depression', 23 May 2012, **psychologylounge.com/stay-at-home-moms-suffer-more-depression**.

5   A.J.C. Torres, L. Barbosa-Silva, L.C. Oliveira-Silva, O.P.P. Miziara, U.C.R. Guahy, A.N. Fisher, and M.K. Ryan, 'The impact of motherhood on women's career progression: A scoping review of evidence-based interventions', *Behavioral Sciences 14:4* (2024), p. 275.

6   Monique Haicault, 'La gestion ordinaire de la vie à deux', *Sociologie du Travail 26:3* (1984), pp. 268–78.

7 Allison Daminger, 'The cognitive dimension of household labor', *American Sociological Review 84:4* (2019), pp. 609–33.

8 Marcus Brotherton, *Teacher: The Henrietta Mears story* (Gospel Light, 2006), p. 82.

9 'Talking Jesus Report 2022: What people in the UK think of Jesus, Christians and evangelism', Evangelical Alliance, **eauk.org/assets/ files/downloads/Talking-Jesus-Report-2022.pdf**.

10 '5 things you need to know gbout Gen Z', 12 September 2024, **barna.com/research/gen-z-2024**.

11 'Sticky faith parents: building lifelong faith', **fulleryouthinstitute. org/stickyfaith/parents**.

12 Zara Hanawalt, 'Why parenting might be your most valuable skill in today's job market', **parents.com/parenting-might-be-your-most- valuable-job-skill-8752192**

Journal pages

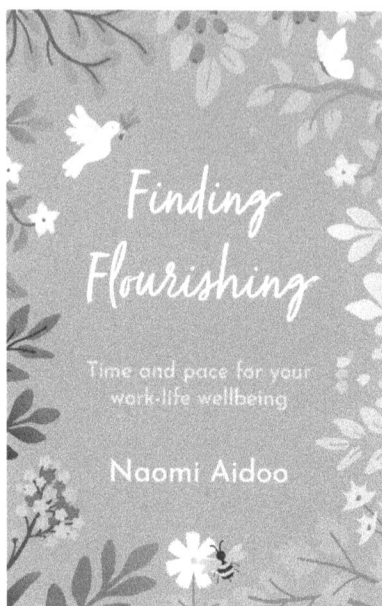

In our fast-paced world, *Finding Flourishing* redefines wellbeing as an accessible daily pursuit, even for the busiest among us. Naomi Aidoo presents a practical and tangible approach to achieving wellbeing, one that doesn't require adding yet another technique to your busy schedule. Instead, it enhances your day-to-day mentally, emotionally and spiritually. This book is an interactive journey with thought-provoking questions, journal prompts, and the opportunity to reflect on daily life from a spiritual perspective, helping you discover a path to everyday wellbeing.

Finding Flourishing
Time and pace for your work-life wellbeing
Naomi Aidoo
978 1 80039 274 8 £8.99

brfonline.org.uk

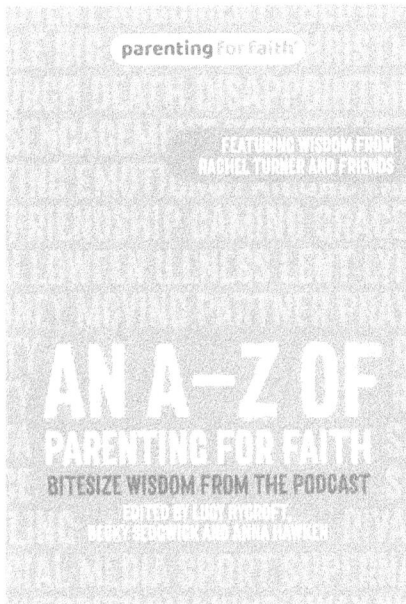

How does a Christian parent tackle common parenting issues? What can we bring to the table that will not only help our children to navigate a complex world, but to do it with faith and a growing awareness of God's presence with them? The Parenting for Faith podcast has been equipping parents since 2018, with over 200 episodes in its back catalogue. This book draws out wisdom from our guests, brought together by the Parenting for Faith team, on 52 relevant topics for parents and carers.

An A–Z of Parenting for Faith
Bitesize wisdom from the podcast
Edited by Lucy Rycroft, Becky Sedgwick, and Anna Hawken
978 1 80039 399 8 £12.99

brfonline.org.uk